LIVING FOᴿ ᴳ

Studies for Disciples in the 21st Century

Melody & Richard Briggs

PiQUANT
editions

British Library Cataloguing in Publication Data
  Briggs, Melody
  Living for God : studies for disciples in the 21st century
  1. Christian life
  I. Title II. Briggs, Richard, 1966-
  248.4

  ISBN-13: 9781903689486

Cover Design by Paul Lewis, LuzDesign

Dedicated to the house groups
that have been our spiritual homes through the years:
chez Chapman, the Rolleston household
the Pathway K groups, the cell groups at St Cuthbert's
and, now, the Light House

Contents

Introduction   vii

SECTION A: Living with God   **1**

Unit I   **Knowing God**   **3**
  1   God the Father   5
  2   God the Son   15
  3   God the Holy Spirit   25
  4   The Trinity   33

Unit II   **The Christian Life**   **43**
  5   What is a Christian?   45
  6   Salvation   53
  7   Being the Church   61
  8   Practicing Faith   69

SECTION B: Hearing from God   **77**

Unit III **The Biblical Story**   **79**
  9   In the Beginning   81
  10   The Story of Israel   89
  11   The Story of Jesus   97
  12   The Early Church and Beyond   105

Unit IV   **Interpreting the Bible**   **113**
  13   Holy Scripture   115
  14   Studying the Bible   123
  15   Reading Poetry and Prophecy   131
     (Psalms & Isaiah)
  16   Reading a Letter (Ephesians)   139

SECTION C: Living in God's World   **149**

    Unit V   Mission—Sharing the Good News   **151**
        17   God's Mission   153
        18   Our Response   161
        19   The Gospel in Context   169
        20   The Uniqueness of Jesus   177

    Unit VI   Christian Hope   **185**
        21   Hope for the Individual   187
        22   Hope for the World   195
        23   Hope for the Future   203
        24   Living with Hope   211

      Suggestions for Further Reading   215
        Resources for Studying the Bible   219
        Useful Reference Works and Textbooks   221

Introduction

Christians are called to love God with all their heart, soul, mind and strength, or, as some people put it, with head, heart and hands:

Head—understanding all we can

Heart—loving with all compassion

Hands—getting involved in practice

Perhaps, above all, we recognize that all of our efforts are really a response:

Responding to God, who has loved us first

This book is a study guide to help us take some steps forward in that process. It is designed for individual or group use. Each study unit can be studied independently of all the others, although we do sometimes refer back or forwards to other studies in the book that contain a further discussion of the same issue.

We hope that you will find the studies both encouraging and challenging: encouraging in helping you see more of the bigger picture of who God is and how God is at work in our lives and in our world; challenging in making you realize how massive a picture that is. It is rightly said that the more we know, the more we realize we do not know. Perhaps as authors we will have been successful if by the end of this book you are frustrated that it does not go further!

The book is aimed at those who are Christians, and who know that they want or need to learn more. We assume that you have a Bible (we generally use the NRSV or NIV in this book), and we generally assume that you have a church, or at least somewhere you can discuss the ideas. We make a few recommendations about other good books that will help you study and reflect, and these are gathered into a section at the end. There is also a recommendation for one particular book for each study. If you obtain these they will be the start of a helpful Christian library.

The material in this study book has been developed from study materials we have used in various settings. Much earlier versions of some of it originally appeared as part of Richard Briggs (ed.), *Global Action: A Personal Discipleship Manual for the World Christian* (Carlisle: OM Publishing, 1997), which was a project developed and sponsored by the interdenominational mission agency Operation Mobilisation (see www.om.org). Although many of the ideas behind that book lie behind this one too, very little of the original text has survived the constant process of reworking this material over the past ten years (and none of the specifically OM copyright material from that edition remains). Our grasp of the issues was refined and refocused when we both had the privilege of teaching, across a range of subjects, in the multicultural environment of All Nations Christian College in Hertfordshire in England, from 1999 to 2003 (www.allnations.ac.uk). Richard taught New Testament, hermeneutics, and even once an Introduction to Christian Theology course. Melody taught church history and New Testament. It was a particular delight that the Foreword to the original *Global Action* book was written by Chris Wright, who was principal at All Nations when we arrived. This background explains another goal of the book: to be a reliable and constructive study manual for Christians around the world in many different cultures and contexts. More recently, Melody has been developing the material in her role training youth and community workers at St John's College, Durham, where she teaches theology as well as mission and community work. We have both also had the chance to teach some of these subjects on the in-church training program at the church we currently attend: Kings Church, Durham.

We are indebted to many—members of OM, students and colleagues at All Nations and friends in Durham—who have helped us by asking excellent questions or frequently pointing out that 'what you have said does not make sense.' We have learned that if something is worth saying it is worth saying clearly, and have tried to follow that rule in this book (although writing about the trinity was a bit of a challenge). Many other people have given us ideas or encouragement along the way. A special thanks to Patricia Briggs for putting together the images of the trinity in Study 4. Although one or the other of us wrote each study individually in the first instance, we have edited the whole book together. This did not stop us having many entertaining conversations along the lines of 'my section is clearer than yours', and we would each like to assure the reader that our co-writer is not infallible.

How the Book is Organized

We have tried to keep the organization of the studies simple. Each of the six study units is divided into four separate studies, making a total of 24 studies. Each study includes the following:

- opening statement of the theme, including the goal of the study
- a Bible passage to read, and questions on the passage to prompt some reflection
- some material on the topic to be studied
- discussion questions and activities for the reader (these are mixed into the study material)

Including all the reading, each study might take about two hours. A group using the book to study together could best operate by making sure that everyone has a copy of the book, with each person reading the Bible passage and the study material ahead of time. Group time can then be spent looking at the study questions and activities. Some of the longer questions with multiple parts could be divided up among different group members who could then report back to the group. In this way the group study might take about one hour for each topic, and could be used as part of a weekly study meeting.

We are happy to receive feedback on your experiences of using this book, especially for group studies. Do please send feedback to us, care of the publisher, Piquant Editions.

We wish you all the best in making use of these studies. May they help you in the exciting and challenging task of living as God's people in God's world today.

Melody and Richard Briggs
Durham, September 2007

Section A

LIVING WITH GOD

UNIT I—KNOWING GOD

I want to know Christ
and the power of his resurrection
and the sharing of his sufferings
by becoming like him in his death,
if somehow I may attain the
resurrection from the dead.

Philippians 3:10–11

We begin, of course, with God.

This unit focuses not just on knowing about God, but also on knowing God. The Greek words for *God (theos)* and *knowing (logos)* combine to give us the word *theology.* In one sense, then, this unit is really a study of theology. Our particular focus is the God of the Christian faith.

STUDIES

1 God the Father

2 God the Son

3 God the Holy Spirit

4 The Trinity

God the Father

Our goal in this study is to ask the basic question: who is God? We will start in the Old Testament, and then see how 'God the Father' is further described in the New Testament.

Bible Passages: Hosea 11:1–11 and John 14:1–14

STUDY QUESTIONS

What do we learn from the Hosea passage about God's relationship with his people?

➢ What does God call Israel in v.1?
➢ How is God described in vv.3–4?
➢ What is Israel's response in v.7?
➢ What do vv.8–9 show us about the state of the relationship?

What do we learn from John 14 about the inseparability of the Father and the Son?

➢ For example, look at the themes of 'accessing', 'knowing', 'seeing' in vv.6,7,9.
➢ What is claimed in v.10? (see also John 10:30)
➢ How else do we bring glory to the Father in this passage?

The Christian God

The first thing to note about the Christian God is that he is one of many 'gods' in the Bible. This God of Israel is described as the true God, in contrast to the gods of other nations. What does this mean? Among other

5

things, it means that the God of Israel is trustworthy, reliable, loving in a way that other gods are not, and a holy God. We will explore many of these ideas in this study, but we start with a simple point about God that is often obscured by our Bible translations. In the Old Testament, the God of Israel had a name. His name identified him as this particular God, not to be confused with any other.

The Name of God

The name of God in the Old Testament is 'YHWH'. This is sometimes called the 'tetragrammaton' (four letters), and like all Hebrew words in the Old Testament it was written down without vowels. The vowels we use today were added in later (see Study 9). In Jewish tradition only the High Priest was allowed to say the name, once a year in the temple. Otherwise, it was replaced by 'the lord' or 'the name', for fear of misusing the name, which is the point of the third of the ten commandments (Exodus 20:7). As a result, we are in the strange position of not really knowing how to pronounce this name.

A common convention was to take the vowels from the word for 'lord' *(adonay)* and add them to the consonants Y + H + W + H. When the Germans did this in the middle ages, they got 'Jehovah'. Twentieth-century scholars suggested that the name 'YHWH', given in Exodus 3:14, is related to the Hebrew verb 'to be' *(ehyeh)*. As a result they suggest that the way to pronounce the word is 'Yahweh', and that it means 'the God who is'. Different traditions have different ways of writing the word today (and Jews would still find it offensive to hear it pronounced):

- Yahweh   —our best scholarly guess
- YHWH (or Yhwh) —to show that the vowels are unknown
- the LORD   —this is the standard English Bible translation technique
- Jehovah   —still in use in the hymns!

In this book we will use 'Yhwh' when we need to make a special reference to this name of God. The Old Testament uses the word 'God' (or 'god') not just for Yhwh, but for many other powers and forces too. The New Testament also does this.

ACTIVITY

Look up the following examples: Deuteronomy 32:8–9, Psalm 82, John 10:31–39, 2 Corinthians 4:4.

What are some of the different ways we (or the culture around us) use the word 'god' today?

The significance of God's name will become clearer when we look at different divine names in the Old Testament:

- *el*   —the basic name for God/a god in the ancient world
- *el elyon*   —God most high (e.g. Genesis 14:17–22)
- *el shaddai* —God Almighty (e.g. Genesis 17:1)
- *elohim*   —common OT word for God/god (and also for 'gods')
- *adonay*   —not a name, but a title ('lord')

Some of the most important Old Testament verses do not make much sense if we do not know this. The only major English translation to keep these names is the *New Jerusalem Bible*, so we quote from that here:

> *God spoke to Moses and said to him, 'I am Yhwh.*
> *To Abraham, Isaac and Jacob I appeared as El*
> *Shaddai, but I did not make my name Yhwh*
> *known to them.'*   (Exodus 6:2–3)

God reveals his name to Moses so that Moses has the authority to confront Pharaoh. Knowing someone's name in the ancient world was important: it meant that you understood who they were (see Genesis 32:22–32 for a story where this matters). A name like 'Elijah' meant 'Yah(weh) is my God *(el)*'.

ACTIVITY

What do your names mean? Are they significant? How did you or would you name a child if you were the parent, and why?

ACTIVITY

Look up some of the following biblical names to see their significance:

Abraham	Naomi	Jesus
Jacob	Christ	Bethel
Israel	Jonathan	Nabal (1 Sam 25:25)
Ruth	Bethlehem	

*Note: You can do this most easily by using any translation (like the NIV) that tells you the meaning of a name in the footnote.

God is the Lord

We noted above that most English Bible translations use 'the LORD' to translate Yhwh. This immediately gives us a particular perspective on who God is. It may be worth pausing and reflecting on this.

ACTIVITY

What associations does the word 'lord' have for me, and how helpful are they?

It is easy to bring into our understanding all kinds of ideas associated with the modern word 'lord' which are not part of the biblical passages where God is revealing who he is. A good example of this is the following passage, again from the *New Jerusalem Bible:*

> *Then Yhwh passed before him and called out,*
> *'Yhwh, Yhwh, God of tenderness and compassion,*
> *slow to anger, rich in faithful love and constancy,*
> *maintaining his faithful love to thousands,*
> *forgiving fault, crime and sin, yet letting nothing*
> *go unchecked, and punishing the parent's fault in*
> *the children and in the grandchildren to the third*
> *and fourth generation.'* (Exodus 34:6–7)

This passage is in many ways telling us who Yhwh is—Yhwh's character and how it will be experienced in Israel.

ACTIVITY

Do these characteristics fit with your associations for the word 'lord'? Work through them one by one and ask: how do they help us to fill out our idea of who God is?

*Note: 'faithful love' (*hesed* in Hebrew) is a very strong word, sometimes translated as 'covenant love' to indicate its sense of commitment.

The reference to 'the third and fourth generation' at the end is perhaps a way of highlighting the effects of the parent's sin 'for as long as he/she is alive', i.e. people will reap the consequences of what they sow their whole life long (rather than saying that their children and grandchildren bear the punishment, except indirectly).

In later Old Testament times, it became common simply to call Yhwh 'Lord' (*adonay*), as we have seen. This tradition goes back to verses like Exodus 23:17 and 34:23 where we read about 'the Lord God' (*yhwh ha'adon*), and in Deuteronomy 10:17 we see Yhwh described as 'the Lord of lords'.

When the Old Testament was translated into Greek, the word 'Lord' became *kurios*, and this is the New Testament word for 'Lord' too. It is therefore very significant that Jesus is described as being given the name *kurios* in Philippians 2:9, and that in 1 Timothy 6:15 we see Jesus called 'the Lord of lords'. Readers of the Old Testament could understand this in only one way: this is a claim that Jesus is somehow the God of the Old Testament. You will have the opportunity to explore this in a later study.

The Lord God: One and Holy

Two particular ways in which God being Lord is to be understood are: God is one, and God is holy. Neither of these is straightforward, although it is easy to quote verses where they are emphasized. The two are probably related. We start with 'God is one':

> *Hear, O Israel: Yhwh our God, Yhwh one.*
> *You must love Yhwh your God with all your*
> *heart, and with all your soul, and with all your*
> *strength.*   (Deuteronomy 6:4–5)

This famous passage is known as the *shema* in Jewish tradition, since the first word of it ('Hear!') is *shema* in Hebrew. It is to be recited and remembered at all times, as the surrounding passage makes clear: it is even to be written on the doorposts of the house, and a copy worn around the forehead. (Feel free to stop and do this as an activity at this point!) The above translation is deliberately strange: it brings out the fact that the opening phrase is very brief ('Yhwh one'). As a result, it can be translated in quite a lot of ways. The NRSV offers the following possibilities:

- the LORD is our God, the LORD alone
- the LORD our God is one LORD
- the LORD our God, the LORD is one
- the LORD is our God, the LORD is one

We cannot settle the debate about how to translate it here. However, it is worth thinking about the purpose of the book of Deuteronomy as a whole. It is presented as Moses' farewell speeches, delivered on the border of the promised land. In fact, in the way the book is written, the whole thing takes place on one day, as a farewell speech from the dying leader. The major theme of these speeches is that Israel is to be holy so that they can enter the land God is giving them, and that when they arrive, they are to find the one key place that Yhwh will show them, and worship there (Deuteronomy 12:13–14). The emphasis is clear, even if the details are not: Israel is to be united as one people before God, in response to the fact that God is one. God's 'oneness' seems to be a way of emphasizing God's superiority (over all other gods), and the fact that God must be worshipped with all Israel's heart and soul and strength.

This is linked to the requirement to be holy, because God is holy, which we find in Leviticus 19:2 (and quoted in the New Testament in 1 Peter 1:16). When the prophet Isaiah has his vision in the temple at the start of his prophetic ministry, he sees the seraphim around God's throne, and they are calling to each other:

> *Holy, holy, holy is Yhwh of hosts (or 'armies')*
> *the whole earth is full of his glory.*   (Isaiah 6:3)

The way to emphasize something in the Old Testament was to repeat it. There are simple examples of this: 'gold' in 2 Kings 25:15 to show how gold the gold was that was being stolen from the temple. It is rare to find anything repeated three times, making this the strongest emphasis of all: God is holy. To be holy is to be 'separate', removed from sin. God can only dwell amongst the people of Israel because Israel is also made holy.

If we say 'God is Lord' (or 'Yhwh is Lord'), then we are saying: God is unique and holy, and this requires us to respond with lives that are set apart for God.

ACTIVITY

In Isaiah 6, in response to his vision of the holiness of God, notice Isaiah's:

—realization that he is lost and unclean (v.5)

—need to have his guilt taken away, since he cannot do it himself (v.7)

—personal response (v.8)

What language could we use today to respond to who God is that would capture the sense of 'one' and 'holy' described above?

The Creator God

Another way the Bible often talks of God is as 'God Almighty'—supreme, incomparable. Consider these words from Isaiah: 'I am the LORD, and there is no other' (Isaiah 45:6) or 'I am He; I am the first, and I am the last' (48:12). This is a picture of a God who did not need to consult anyone in the work of the creation of the world (40:12–14). Instead, 'Yhwh is the everlasting God, the Creator of the ends of the earth' (40:28).

This testimony to God as creator is obviously in Genesis 1 as well. In contrast to many other ancient stories about how the world began, the Genesis account is simple and straightforward. There are no tales of different gods all battling each other to see who would win. The God of the Old Testament is the only God in view at the beginning of Genesis. He creates everything in its place, according to its kind, in a structured and systematic way. It is as if the opening chapter of the Bible wants to tell us that the world is a fundamentally good and ordered place, because God has set it in motion in just the way he wanted it.

In the New Testament, the creator God is described as making not just the visible world, but 'all things in heaven and earth ... visible and invisible' (Colossians 1:15).

The God of the Bible is a God who takes great delight in his creation: everything he sees is 'good' throughout Genesis 1.

ACTIVITY

Read Psalm 19:1–6 for a description of how the creation reflects its creator. How have you experienced God's goodness in the created world around you?

Father God

The extraordinary tension of the biblical picture of God is that this holy and unique Lord wants nothing more than a covenant relationship with his people. From the fact that this is not a smooth relationship flows most of the story of the Old Testament.

The God of Israel is the God who is a Father to his people. This is the background to Jesus being called 'the Son' in the New Testament: he is the Son because the God that he is revealing is the Father, and their relationship is described in Father-Son language. This is very clear in John's gospel.

A final passage that is very important here is Ephesians 3:14–15. Here we read that 'every family in heaven and on earth takes its name' from the Father. There is a word-play in the Greek of this verse that ties together the 'Father' and the 'family' on earth which is named after him. The key point is this: we know what it means to have a human father because we first have a heavenly Father. In our life experience we tend to think about this the other way around: we know our 'father' and then think 'God must be like that.' The point of the Ephesians verse is to remind us that we should not model our relationship with God after our human relationships, but should model our human relationships after who God is.

ACTIVITY

Just as with 'Lord' earlier, it is important that we work out what the word 'Father' means in terms of the biblical picture. Most of us will start from a basic image provided by our own (human) father: take some time to note down what sort of image this is. Now ask yourself how to fill your image of 'father' with the biblical picture of God. You many find it useful to refer back to your studies of Hosea 11 and John 14.

We have reached the point where we are ready to go on to our next topic, 'God the Son', to continue to explore who God is.

God the Son

We turn next to God the Son: Jesus. Here we will consider Jesus' identity, personhood and the nature of his incarnation, beginning with a passage that brings some of these ideas into focus.

Bible Passage: Philippians 2:5–11

STUDY QUESTIONS

What do you learn from this passage about the incarnation of Christ?

➢ What is the form or nature of God? (v.6)

➢ What is the form or nature of a slave? (v.7)

➢ Why did Jesus become human?

➢ What does it mean to be obedient to death? (v.8)

➢ Is it that every tongue will confess, or that every tongue might (be able to) confess, and what's the difference? (v.11)

➢ What is the ultimate result of Jesus' humility and obedience?

Jesus' Identity

Before considering Jesus' identity, it is helpful to think through how we understand our own identities, and identity in general.

ACTIVITY

Consider for a moment: Who are you?

ACTIVITY

If you are working through this study in a group, divide into pairs and ask each other this question: who are you? Keep a record of your responses. If you are working alone, pause to answer this question on paper, in a paragraph or less.

Next, assess your answer. How did you answer the question? Did you separate out identity, responsibilities and relationships, or were they intertwined?

Understanding the identity of Jesus—who he is—is inseparable from understanding what he does. In other words, Jesus' identity and function are inseparable. We recognize Jesus through what he has done, and particularly through his impact upon our lives. It is impossible to speak of someone's identity apart from their personal history, their life story.

When the early church proclaimed Jesus it did so by telling his life story, which is basically what the gospels are—ancient forms of biography. This gospel message encompassed the identity, the life and the work of Jesus. In one sense, Jesus is the gospel.

ACTIVITY

Take a moment to read Acts 10:34–43 as an example of the proclamation of the gospel by the early church. How is Jesus described in this passage?

*Note: It has been claimed that Peter's speech here is the kind of testimony to Jesus that Mark used in writing his gospel. You might note how this sermon captures the outline of Mark's gospel.

Jesus is at the centre of the Christian faith. Christianity started with Jesus, initiated through his life, death and resurrection. On the one hand this makes Christianity a historical religion, originating as it does in a person rather than a set of abstract ideas. On the other hand the biblical witness is not primarily concerned to inform us about history, that a man named Jesus once lived or did and said certain things. Rather, the New Testament makes a claim about the purpose of these things: it proclaims Jesus as the bearer of salvation. Salvation comes through his life, death and resurrection, for in Jesus, God is acting for the salvation of the world.

ACTIVITY

If somebody asked you 'Who is Jesus?' how would you answer them? What would your answer say about Jesus' identity and his actions?

Scripture attributes a variety of titles to Jesus, all of which reflect some aspect of his identity. Perhaps the most fundamental of these is:

- *Messiah*—from the Hebrew word that means 'one who has been anointed', and used to refer to a king anointed by God. The Greek translation for this word is *Christos,* that is, 'Christ'.

Anointing is a public sign of being chosen by God for a task. Yet the term 'Messiah' was also linked to a particular set of expectations in Israel, expectations of a coming King who would ultimately and irrevocably overthrow all those who oppress God's chosen people. The title 'Messiah' establishes Jesus' relationship to Israel. He is the fulfilment of Jewish prophecy, and on him hinges the continuity between Judaism and Christianity. The Old Testament, the Scriptures of the Jewish people, is fundamental to an understanding of 'Messiah'.

ACTIVITY

Look at some of the passages in the Old Testament that are sometimes called Messianic prophecies, e.g. Psalm 22:1–18, Isaiah 9:2–9, 53:1–12. What sort of portrait of the Messiah do these passages paint?

In the Jewish mind, nationalism and messianic expectations became linked. During the Roman occupation of Palestine in the first century BC, these expectations were high. Many of Jesus' contemporaries expected a victorious, conquering Messiah, not a suffering one. Jesus, in contrast, did not regard himself as a nationalist Messiah. When Peter confesses that he is the Messiah, Jesus affirms his insight and then tells the disciples to keep it a secret! The way Mark tells this in Mark 8:27–30 has sometimes been called the story of a 'messianic secret'.

ACTIVITY

Read Mark 8:27–30. Why do you think this secrecy may have been necessary?

Another title for Jesus is:

- *Son of Man*—this is Jesus' most common way of referring to himself, and there is much debate about its meaning, but perhaps one point was that Jesus was affirming his humanity.

This term has its roots in the 7th chapter of the book of Daniel, in a vision about how God ('the Ancient of Days') will judge the kingdoms of the world and give an everlasting kingdom to God's people ('the people of the holy ones of the Most High', Daniel 7:27). In that context, the phrase 'one like a son of man' (7:13) appears to emphasize a human figure (in the midst of a vision of angels, beasts and so forth) who is given authority over God's people.

Perhaps Jesus used the term to indicate that he was fulfilling the calling of Israel to be God's servant on behalf of all the nations. Jesus' human identity embraces unity with other people, especially the weak and humble. 'Son of Man' indicates the suffering Jesus experiences for the sake of humanity.

- *Son of God,* by contrast, affirms Jesus' divinity. While Jesus does not explicitly use this term of himself, the title is applied to Jesus by a variety of New Testament writers.

In the Old Testament, sonship refers, at times, to the people of Israel (Exodus 4:22), but primarily to the Davidic king and his successors (2 Samuel 7:14). For the New Testament authors, the Son of God is a term used exclusively for Jesus.

ACTIVITY

Take a moment to read Daniel 7:9–14 and Mark 8:31–32 for references to the Son of Man. Then read 2 Samuel 7:11b–16 and Hebrews 4:14–16 for references to the Son of God. Note that the passage in 2 Samuel is a prophecy.

- Lord *(kyrios)*—in Study 1 you saw how this term was used as an equivalent to 'Yhwh' when the Old Testament was translated into Greek.

In other words, *kyrios* was reserved for God and by using this term, Jesus and his followers identify him with God. One of the earliest Christian confessions of faith was 'Jesus is Lord'.

ACTIVITY

Read Romans 10:9 and 1 Corinthians 12:3 for examples of the confession 'Jesus is Lord'. See also Luke 20:41–44 for an example of Jesus referring to himself as Lord. What are some of the implications of calling Jesus 'Lord'?

The early church drew Jesus' multi-faceted identity together in the label, *ichthus*. This word, which means 'fish' in Greek (ιχθνς) functioned as an acronym. Each letter of *ichthus* represents a title of Jesus:

- ι (i)   —*Iesous*   Jesus
- χ (ch) —*Christos*   Christ
- θ (th) —*theos*   God's
- υ (u)   —*uios*   Son
- ς (s)   —*soter*   Saviour

The fish became a symbol of faith in the early church, and a shorthand way of indicating what they believed about their Lord. A simple fish symbol is still used today in some settings.

Jesus as a Person: Human and Divine

Calling Jesus 'Son of God' and 'Son of Man' indicates that his personhood embraces both divinity and humanity, and indeed the biblical portrayal of Jesus' personhood emphasizes both.

Jesus' humanity is testified to in passages that discuss his birth and ancestry, as well as in those displaying evidence of human frailty, such as physical weakness and temptation. His genealogy, birth and childhood indicate that he was part of a human family and underwent the normal process of human development. Displays of emotion, such as joy (Luke 10:21) and sorrow (Matthew 26:37), as well as signs of physical weakness, such as weariness (John 4:6) and hunger (Matthew 21:18), mark Jesus as subject to the vicissitudes of human life. He was even tempted to sin (Luke 4:1–13). Jesus' weaknesses and temptation ensure his identification with us: 'we do not have a high priest who is unable to sympathize with our weaknesses, but we have one who in every respect has been tempted as we are, yet without sin' (Hebrews 4:15). Significantly, Jesus also experienced physical pain and death (Mark 15:16–37).

ACTIVITY

How do some of the following passages testify to Jesus' humanity? Matthew 1:1–6, Luke 2:7, Luke 2:40–52; Matthew 26:37, John 4:6, Matthew 11:19 and Matthew 4:1–11. If you are working in a group, each person could prepare a different passage.

Jesus' divinity is testified to in passages that label him as divine as well as those which identify him with the God of Israel. Jesus performs tasks that God alone can perform. This is especially noticeable in the story about Jesus forgiving sins (Mark 2:1–12). The response of the Jewish leaders in v.7 makes the point clear. Significantly, he receives worship which is due for God alone, and which would be in direct breach of the first commandment (Exodus 20:3) if Jesus were not God.

It is debatable how far the New Testament explicitly calls Jesus God. Romans 9:5 comes close, but it all depends where you put the comma (!) and scholars cannot agree on that. 2 Peter 1:1 calls Jesus 'our God and Saviour', again depending on how it is translated. The clearest indications come in John's gospel, especially in the links between John 1:1 and John 1:14, where the 'Word' *(logos)* who is God becomes flesh, in Jesus. In John 20:28, Thomas confesses Jesus as 'my Lord and my God'. And Jesus himself uses self-designations, such as 'I am' (John 8:58), which identify him with Yhwh, the God of Israel.

ACTIVITY

Now look for testimony of Jesus' divinity in John 1:1–18, Romans 9:5, Hebrews 1:8, Exodus 3:14 and John 8:58; Isaiah 43:11; Matthew 1:21 and Acts 4:12; Colossians 1:16–18, 2:9; Matthew 28:17–18; Titus 2:13; Revelation 5:12–14.

Because Jesus is fully God and fully human, he reveals God to humanity. That is, Jesus is God's self-revelation. As Jesus says to Philip, 'he who has seen me has seen the Father' (John 14:9). This revelation is historical and personal: Jesus reveals God and not merely ideas about God. Therefore, faith in Jesus entails a personal encounter with God.

An examination of the person of Christ broadens our understanding of God. The gospel story redefines the meaning of divinity by showing the actions and sufferings of a humble servant. In Jesus, God serves people, suffers for people and then triumphs, not politically or economically but over death, the enemy of humanity. By looking at Jesus, we know God more fully.

Incarnation

The word 'incarnation' means 'becoming flesh'. The incarnation, by definition, is the uniting of humanity and deity in the person of Jesus Christ. As you saw above, Jesus was both fully human and fully God. But, you may ask, how did this work? This is a good question, and it vexed the early church, leading to a variety of theories. Many of these were eventually rejected and in AD451 the church formulated the 'Chalcedonian Definition', which expresses the boundaries within which an orthodox understanding of the incarnation must operate. Most church traditions adhere to this creed. It is reproduced on page 22.

The guiding principle was this: provided that it is recognized that Jesus is both truly divine and truly human, the precise manner in which his personhood is articulated or explored is not of fundamental importance. According to this creed, the incarnation was a perfectly integrated union of two separate natures (human and divine) in one person, so that neither nature was changed (this is called a 'hypostatic union' in theological discussion). Ultimately, the unity of Jesus' person was and is acknowledged as a mystery. The *purpose* of the incarnation, however, is clearer.

ACTIVITY

What was the purpose of the incarnation and why was Jesus' humanity and divinity necessary to that purpose? If you are working in a group, take a few minutes to discuss this question. If you are working on your own, write down your thoughts in a paragraph or two.

The Definition of Chalcedon

Therefore, following the holy fathers,
we all with one accord
teach men to acknowledge one and the same Son,
our Lord Jesus Christ,
at once complete in Godhead
and complete in manhood,
truly God and truly man,
consisting also of a reasonable soul and body;
of one substance with the Father as regards his
Godhead,
and at the same time of one substance with us
as regards his manhood;

like us in all respects,
apart from sin;
as regards his Godhead,
begotten of the Father before the ages,
but yet as regards his manhood begotten,
for us men and for our salvation,
of Mary the Virgin, the God-bearer;

one and the same Christ, Son, Lord, Only-begotten,
recognized in two natures,
without confusion, without change,
without division, without separation:
the distinction of natures being in no way annulled
by the union,
but rather the characteristics of each nature being
preserved
and coming together to form one person and
subsistence,
not as parted or separated into two persons,
but one and the same Son
and Only-begotten God the Word,
Lord Jesus Christ;

even as the prophets from earliest times spoke of him,
and our Lord Jesus Christ himself taught us,
and the creed of the fathers handed down to us.

Hebrews 2:14–17 indicates that the humanity of Jesus enables him not only to identify with humanity, but also to provide salvation. The salvation of humanity, through Christ's death and resurrection, depends upon his full humanity, for, in the words of the fourth-century Bishop of Constantinople, Gregory of Nazianzus (329–390), 'what has not been assumed has not been healed; it is what is united to his divinity that is saved.'

Through Jesus' incarnation, divinity assumes full humanity, enabling salvation to permeate every aspect of human existence.

If anyone has put their trust in him as a human being lacking a human mind, they are themselves mindless and not worthy of salvation. For what has not been assumed has not been healed; it is what is united to his divinity that is saved... Let them not grudge us our total salvation, or endue the Saviour only with the bones & nerves and mere appearance of humanity.

Gregory of Nazianzus

God the Holy Spirit

Now we will consider God the Spirit. In this study, you will think about biblical images of the Spirit as well as the Spirit's role in our lives.

Bible Passage: Romans 8:1–27

STUDY QUESTIONS

What do we learn from this passage about the Holy Spirit?

➢ What contrasts does Paul make between living by the flesh and living by the Spirit? Why are the two incompatible? (vv.1–13)

➢ How does Paul describe those who have the Spirit? (vv.15–17)

➢ Paul suggests that human beings receiving the Spirit are the 'first fruits' of a bigger project (vv.18–25). What is this project?

➢ What is the Spirit's role in prayer? (vv.26–27)

Biblical Images of the Spirit

What do you think is the significance of the Spirit in the Christian life?

ACTIVITY

What if the Christian faith only had the Father and the Son? What would we miss?

Asking this question helps us to see why the Spirit is important to our faith. Without the Spirit, we would have God, but we would remain separate from him. The key aspect of the role of the Spirit in our lives is this: we are united to God by the Spirit. That is, God is in us through his Spirit. As

Martin Luther (1483–1546) put it, 'of what help is it to you that God is God, if he is not God to you?'

The Spirit is known as the 'Holy Spirit' and the word 'holy' means 'set apart'. This Spirit is not like any other spirit. In the New Testament we find the claim that God is Spirit, as in John 4:24 and 2 Corinthians 3:17. The Holy Spirit is God at work in the world, setting apart people, God's church, for the kingdom.

The words for 'spirit' in the Bible (*rûach* in Hebrew, *pneuma* in Greek) have a variety of uses. *Rûach* can mean spirit, breath of life, storm wind, vitality, or something like 'soul'. It connotes the presence of energy, activity and power (see Micah 3:8). A variety of images portray the Spirit as an invisible, but dynamic energy—the power of God. Genesis 2:7 and Ezekiel 37:9–10, for instance, describe the Spirit as the 'life-breath'—that is, the Spirit is the principle and source of life.

In the Old Testament, God's Spirit is at times depicted with imagery associated with the wind, as in Genesis 1:2. Jesus picks up on this image in his discussion of the Spirit in John 3:8. Other images of the Spirit include:

- fire—as in Isaiah 4:4 and 33:11, Matthew 3:11–13, Luke 12:49 and Acts 2:3

- water—a symbol for wisdom, as in Isaiah 32:15 and 44:3, John 4:10, 23 and 7:38–39 and Revelation 22:1–2

- a dove—at Jesus' baptism, for instance in Matthew 3:16

ACTIVITY

Look up the passages listed above. If you are working in a group, have each person investigate a different image. What does each image contribute to an understanding of the Spirit?

Images of the Spirit such as wind, fire and water are mostly impersonal. Further biblical accounts build on these, showing the Spirit's personal nature. Building on the image of the Spirit as life-breath, the Spirit is consistently portrayed in Scripture as the giver of life. In Genesis 1:2 the Spirit is present at the beginning of creation while in Genesis 2:7 the breath of God initiates life at the creation of humanity. Then in Luke 1:35, the Spirit initiates Jesus' conception. In Acts 2, the Spirit births the church. The church is the work of the Spirit and Pentecost marks the beginning of a new epoch in the history of human life. Since Pentecost, all of God's people experience life in God.

The Spirit may be described as 'God in action', an action that includes saving and empowering. The Spirit is the source of power at creation and the Spirit empowers Jesus' ministry. The descent of the Spirit at Jesus' baptism, in Luke 3:21 for instance, inaugurates a new era in which Jesus not only proclaims but also demonstrates the kingdom of God as he heals, casts out demons and feeds the hungry. The coming of the Spirit at Pentecost brings this salvation into the lives of Jesus' followers.

Of course, the Spirit is also a gift from God (Acts 2:38 and Hebrews 6:4). In the Old Testament, people who received this gift and were filled with the Spirit were often—although not exclusively—prophets, as in Isaiah 61:1 and Ezekiel 2:1–2. As the Spirit of prophecy, the Spirit functions as a channel of communication between God and his people. The Spirit also empowered leaders, such as Moses (Numbers 11:17,29), David (1 Samuel 16:13) and the judges (Judges 3:10, 6:34, 11:29), as well as craftsmen (Exodus 28:3ff) to do the work of God. The Old Testament prophecy of the Spirit coming upon all of God's people, in Joel 2:28–29, is fulfilled at Pentecost, when God pours his Spirit out upon all of his followers.

ACTIVITY

Read Joel 2:28–29, and then Acts 2:1–33 for both the prophecy and Peter's account of how this prophecy has been fulfilled.

A final image of the Spirit can be found in John 14–16, where Jesus calls the Spirit the *paraclete*. This Greek term refers to someone who offers counsel, support or help, connoting a person who provides official assistance. The *paraclete* continues Jesus' ministry after his ascension, mediating the presence of God to believers (John 14:16–17,26; 15:26–27; 16:7–15). This does not, however, lead to a distant Messiah, for the Spirit is the 'Spirit of Christ' (Romans 8:9). Through the Spirit, the believer experiences Christ's presence.

According to John 16:7, Jesus ascends so that the Spirit might descend upon and indwell his followers. Jesus thus prophesies Pentecost. Through this indwelling, the Spirit will both interpret and continue Jesus' teaching (John 14:26, 16:12–15). The writing of the New Testament may be seen as partial fulfilment of this prophecy. Also, the *paraclete* provides an on-going witness to Jesus, particularly by sending those he indwells into the world to provide testimony (John 15:26–27).

ACTIVITY

Examine these passages on the paraclete: John 14:15–26, 15:26–27, and 16:4b–15. Notice how discussion of the Spirit is mixed with discussion of the on-going role of the disciples. How is this particular image of the Spirit relevant to Jesus' teaching here?

The Role of the Spirit

What does the Spirit do? Bishop John V. Taylor described the Spirit as 'the Go-Between God'. The Spirit mediates human relationship with both Father and Son. In Galatians 4:6, the Spirit in the heart of believers' cries 'Abba! Father!' Paul similarly asserts in 1 Corinthians 12:3 that the believer's ability to declare 'Jesus is Lord' comes from the Spirit. The Spirit brings the personal presence of the Godhead into the lives of believers.

The Spirit likewise enables relationship within the church. It is the Spirit who initiates the church at Pentecost and sustains community. It is the Spirit who unites the body (1 Corinthians 12:12–13)—believers are united not only to Christ but also to each other. As will be seen in the following study, the trinity exists as a divine community of being. The church is meant to reflect this fellowship found in the Godhead.

It is the Spirit who gives gifts to God's people for 'building up the body of Christ, until all of us come to the unity of the faith and of the knowledge of the Son of God, to maturity, to the measure of the full stature of Christ' (Ephesians 4:12b–13). The purpose of the gifts of the Spirit is *for other members of the body*. The Spirit empowers Christians to edify one another.

ACTIVITY

A similar point could be made about the fruit of the Spirit. Take a moment to read Galatians 5:22–26. Fruit such as gentleness, kindness and patience are best demonstrated through relationships with other people.

Paul in 2 Corinthians 3:17 asserts 'where the Spirit of the Lord is, there is freedom'. The believer's relationship with God occurs through the Spirit's liberating power. Freedom from what? Bondage to sin and the world. Freedom for what? To be like Christ and to serve God in the world. The entrance of the Spirit into our mortal bodies brings life, forming a new creation through inward renewal of the individual.

To be in relationship with the Father and Son is life. Both Jeremiah and Ezekiel prophesy a new covenant in which God will place his Spirit in people (Jeremiah 31:31–34 and Ezekiel 36:23–28). In 2 Corinthians 3:3–18, Paul claims that this prophecy has been fulfilled in Christ with the coming of the Spirit. Here the work of the Spirit stands in contrast to the work of the law. The Spirit enables obedience where the written law could not. This new covenant is written, not on stone, but on pliable human hearts, etched into the life of each believer.

Jesus declares that the gift of the Spirit is for those who believe (John 14:17). Although non-believers may not experience the indwelling of the Spirit, this does not limit the work of the Spirit to responsive human vessels. There is a cosmic dimension to the Spirit's work. The work of the Spirit is characterized by that which enhances life and peace and which battles against the forces of destruction and death in the world.

Sanctification

The Spirit, then, enables relationship with God. Like all true relationships, this one is two-way. You receive salvation and a new life, and, in response you give your trust and worship. The Spirit glorifies Jesus (John 16:14) by enabling the church to worship its Saviour. Prayer, as conversation with God, exemplifies the two-way nature of the relationship. In prayer you both speak to God and hear from God.

Those in relationship invariably influence one another, and this is true of our relationship with God. Exposure to God means exposure to holiness, a holiness that penetrates our lives. This penetration of the believer's life is called sanctification and is the work of the Spirit. Sanctification means, quite simply, 'to make holy', or, as you saw earlier, to be set apart for God. It has not only ethical implications, but also implications for direction and life purpose. It is the Spirit who enables the believer to live for God. Sanctification refers to the way in which you become Christ-like, on a day-to-day level. As John Calvin (1509–64) described it, sanctification is the 'application of salvation'. It is a life-long process.

Paul calls the Spirit a seal marking out God's people. In this, the Spirit functions as God's mark of ownership on our lives, as well as God's guarantee of our redemption.

ACTIVITY

Read Ephesians 1:13–14, 4:30 and 2 Corinthians 1:21–22 for descriptions of the Spirit as God's seal. What does the image of a seal indicate about the role of the Spirit in your life?

To live in the Spirit is to be transformed into the likeness of Christ. The Spirit shapes us to be like Jesus, transforming us into the image of God (2 Corinthians 3:18), an image seen most clearly in Christ. This transformation makes us more fully human as we gradually reflect more fully the creatures God intended us to be.

This means that the Christian life is not static. Transformation is a process. It often occurs in stages and the alterations are rarely smooth. Many of them may be painful. Most of us experience periods of slow growth interspersed with leaps forward as we submit our understanding, and our sin, to the Spirit. Conviction about sin and strength to denounce it are part of this process. The Spirit stands in opposition to our sinful nature, sustaining the believer in the battle against sin.

ACTIVITY

Read Galatians 5:16–26 for Paul's contrast of the work of the Spirit with the work of the sinful nature in our lives.

The fruit of the Spirit is a sign of the Spirit transforming the believer. Yielding to the Spirit produces these moral virtues, while refusing to yield stops them from growing. The believer cannot have it both ways: sin spoils the fruit.

This tension between Spirit and sinful inclination continues throughout the life of the believer, for our current bodies bear the image of Adam, that is, the taint of sin (1 Corinthians 15:49). We will live in a body of death until the resurrection of believers when our bodies will be redeemed

(Romans 8:23). The process of sanctification could, in fact, be described as the process of preparing us for our resurrection bodies and for resurrection life in the kingdom. Through the Spirit, the resurrection life has invaded our present and works for our future. This orientation towards the future, towards God's kingdom, produces hope.

ACTIVITY

Take a moment to consider the work of the Spirit in your own life. In what ways do you think that the Spirit is preparing you for the kingdom? If appropriate, you may want to spend some time in prayer, bringing this consideration before God.

The Divinity of the Spirit

Before concluding this study, we should spend a few moments considering the divinity of the Spirit. How do we know that the Spirit is a member of the Godhead? In our next study we will consider the trinity as a whole, so brief consideration here of the Spirit's divinity will prepare the ground.

Arguments for the Spirit's divinity rest with a variety of factors. The traditional baptismal formula used in the church comes from Matthew 28:17–20, where Jesus tells his followers to make new disciples and to baptize them 'in the name of the Father and of the Son and of the Holy Spirit'. This formula essentially treats the Three as One.

ACTIVITY

Father, Son and Spirit are also united in Paul's benediction in 2 Corinthians 13:13. Take a moment to look at this verse. What is the Spirit's distinct contribution, here, to the lives of believers?

Scripture attributes divine titles to the Spirit. In 2 Corinthians 4:17, the Spirit is Lord. Paul refers to the Spirit as God's Spirit in 1 Corinthians 2:14 and as the Spirit of Christ in Romans 8:9, while in 1 Corinthians 2:10–11 he argues that only the Spirit can know—and reveal—the things of God. Similarly, the Spirit performs functions of God, initiating life, guiding the development of the church and sanctifying believers.

The church fathers pointed out that the Spirit is the source of holiness in the lives of believers. Such holiness must come from the divine nature, and not from an external source, in order to be effective.

> *Only a divine Spirit could make us partakers of a divine nature.*
>
> Basil of Caesarea (330-379)

The Trinity

We conclude this unit with a study of the trinity. Having looked at God the Father, Son and Spirit separately, it is time to consider their unity.

Bible Passage: Ephesians 1:3–14

STUDY QUESTIONS

What is the role of the Father in salvation?

➤ What are the benefits of the Father's grace and how do we receive it? (vv.6–8)

What is the role of the Son in salvation?

➤ How does the Son fulfil the plans of the Father?

What is the role of the Holy Spirit in salvation? (vv.13–14)

➤ What is our inheritance?

Three Yet One

God the Father, God the Son and God the Holy Spirit are not separate deities but one God, a concept expressed through the term 'trinity'. This word 'trinity' (from the Latin *trinitas*) was coined by the second-century African theologian Tertullian as a means of articulating the nature of the Godhead.

ACTIVITY

Consider your personal understanding of the trinity. Jot down briefly your own definition.

The Nicene Creed

We believe in one God
the Father Almighty,
maker of heaven and earth,
and of all things visible and invisible.

And in one Lord Jesus Christ,
the only-begotten Son of God,
Begotten of the Father before all the ages,
Light of Light,
True God of true God
begotten not made,
of one substance with the Father,
through whom all things were made,
who for us men and our salvation
came down from the heavens,
and was made flesh of the Holy Spirit
and the Virgin Mary,
and became man,
and was crucified for us under Pontius Pilate,
and suffered and was buried,
and rose again on the third day according to the
Scriptures,
and ascended into the heavens,
and sits on the right hand of the Father,
and shall come again with glory to judge living and
dead
of whose kingdom there shall be no end.

And in the Holy Spirit,
the Lord and the Life-giver,
that proceeds from the Father,
who with Father and Son is worshipped together
and glorified together,
who spoke through the prophets.

We believe in one holy catholic and apostolic church.

We acknowledge one baptism for the remission of sins.
We look for the resurrection of the dead,
and the life of the age to come.

The key idea of the doctrine of the trinity is this:

• God is one being yet three eternally distinct persons.

The source of unity of the Godhead is the single divine essence of which the Godhead consists. Yet within this one essence are three eternal, not temporary, persons.

The English term 'person' can be misleading for it implies that each member of the Godhead is a distinct, separate individual. But within the trinity, 'person' does not mean an individual; that is, God is not three individuals. The problem arises through a loss of meaning in translation. 'Person' actually translates the Latin word, *persona*, a legal term referring to social roles; this word was particularly used to discuss people in terms of their identification with other people. Thus *persona* refers to a person within a community in which life is shared and mutually exchanged among a variety of people. A *persona* shares in the lives of others, in marked contrast to the sense in which a contemporary Western 'person' is an autonomous (independent) individual.

The unity of the three persons leads to the use of the word 'triune' (three-in-one) to describe God. God is a triune community of being, where all members of the Godhead share the same essence, but are three because they are different *personae* in relation to each other. The substance unites while the *persona* distinguishes.

The fourth-century church, in response to a variety of assertions about the nature of the trinity, devised a statement of doctrine for the trinity. This statement, known as the Nicene Creed, is accepted in all branches of the Christian church. It is reproduced on page 34.

ACTIVITY

Read through the creed. Which member of the Godhead receives the most attention? Why might that be? What sorts of things are emphasized?

The Nicene Creed was written in response to a particular issue and therefore reflects the specific context of the fourth-century church. The creed asserts the eternality of Christ, in reaction to the theological debate raging at that time. While it does state the divinity of the Spirit, the nature of the Holy Spirit was not the focus issue. Like the Definition of Chalcedon, discussed in Study 2, the Nicene Creed seeks to provide boundaries within which theological discussion can operate. Therefore this creed does not address all areas of concern relevant to the trinity. For instance, it does not discuss how an eternal God could suffer or experience death. It provides guidelines for understanding rather than a conclusive explanation of how it all works.

The Trinity in Scripture

The foundation of the doctrine of the trinity is in the Bible, but it is not fully developed or stated. You have seen in Studies 1, 2 and 3 how Scripture testifies to the divinity of Father, Son and Holy Spirit, while simultaneously proclaiming a faith in one creator God and Lord. Father, Son and Holy Spirit are mentioned together in both Matthew 28:19 and 2 Corinthians 13:13, in a way which already seems to suggest an equality between them. All three members of the Godhead are clearly present at Jesus' baptism (Matthew 3:16–17) while passages such as John 14:15–26, Acts 2:32–33, and Ephesians 1:3–14 and 3:14–19 strongly imply God's triune nature. (Note: some old translations include a verse in 1 John 5:7 which says that the Father, Son and Spirit are one, but there is very little evidence for this verse in the oldest Greek manuscripts—it was added in at the time of Erasmus in the sixteenth century.)

ACTIVITY

Read the passages listed in the paragraph above. How are Father, Son and Holy Spirit viewed in each instance?

Read 1 Corinthians 8:4–6 and compare it with the *shema* in Deuteronomy 6:4–5 (see Study 1). What do you notice? How does Paul explain the 'one-ness' of God?

The Old Testament contains glimpses of God's triune nature. The Spirit of God is active in passages such as Genesis 1:2, Psalm 139:7 and Isaiah 63:10–14. The Word of God is personalized in passages such as Psalm 33:6,9 (compare John 1:1–3). Sometimes New Testament authors draw out an additional perspective: for example, John treats Isaiah's vision of God as a vision of Jesus (John 12:36b–41; compare Isaiah 53:1 and 6:10).

ACTIVITY

Pause for a moment to read through the passages mentioned in the paragraph above.

Divine acts, such as creation, are attributed to all three members of the Godhead. The Father initiates creation (Genesis 1:1), through the Spirit (Genesis 1:2) and the Word (Psalm 33:6, John 1:3). The passage examined at the beginning of this study further clarifies the roles of the Godhead. Regarding humanity's salvation, Ephesians 1:3–14 indicates that the Father elects, the Son redeems and the Spirit seals God's people for the completion of that redemption. Stating their roles succinctly, the Father is revealed to humanity in Christ through the Spirit.

Exploring the Doctrine of the Trinity

There is no easy way to understand the trinity, no surprise explanation that we haven't heard before that will make it all seem suddenly simple. It took the early church centuries to work out what exactly we can and cannot say about the three-in-one God. We can learn some helpful things, however, from seeing how they thought through the doctrine of the trinity. There are two important points to note.

- Firstly, the doctrine was to be grounded in humanity's need for salvation, as testified to in the drama of salvation in Scripture.
- Secondly, it was easier to say what the trinity was not, rather than what it was.

A view of a doctrine 'other' than the orthodox one is known as a 'heresy' (deriving from a Greek word for 'other'), and such a view is known as 'heretical'. So in fact looking at early heresies can help us follow the church's arguments: it allows us to establish boundaries within which the trinity can be understood. We begin, then, with two heretical ideas that should help us to further clarify the nature of the trinity.

The early church wrestled with maintaining monotheism while simultaneously worshipping both God the Father and Jesus. One solution presented in the late second century was a belief called modalism. According to modalism, God is one deity who appears to humanity in three temporary forms or 'modes'. First God appeared as creator, then as redeemer, and finally as sustainer; or, God manifested himself first as Father, then as Son and finally as the Spirit. Thus Father, Son and Spirit are three names attached to one God. Essentially God takes on different forms—or puts on different masks—at different times in human history.

ACTIVITY

Can you think of reasons why people might have thought this? Can you see any problems with it?

Scripture testifies to the co-existence of Father, Son and Holy Spirit. As you saw above, all three are present at Jesus' baptism (Matthew 3:16–17). In Gethsemane, Jesus prays to the Father (Mark 14:35–36) and following his ascension, he sits at the right hand of God (Colossians 3:1). Modalism simplifies the biblical idea of God to try and make it easier to understand. The idea lives on today when people try to illustrate the trinity by saying that it is a bit like having ice, which then melts and becomes water, which then evaporates and becomes steam. This might illustrate how one substance can be in three 'modes', but the Father, Son and Spirit are not simply manifestations of God occurring at different times.

Not only do Father, Son and Spirit co-exist, but they are also eternal. Another early church heresy, Arianism, denied that Jesus was eternal. According to Arianism, Jesus is from God, but not of God. Arians argued that since the Father 'gave birth' to the Son, the Son had a beginning. (Note that in response to this the creeds say that Jesus was 'begotten not made'—in other words he is eternally the Son.) They thought that Jesus was therefore pre-existent, brought into existence by the Father before the creation of the world, but not eternal. Jesus was God's Son by the will of God, but not by nature since he was not of the same substance as God. Consequently, the Son was subordinate to the Father.

ACTIVITY

Arians used passages like John 14:28, 1 Corinthians 15:28 and Colossians 1:15 to defend their position. Their opponents used passages like Hebrews 13:8, 1 Corinthians 8:6 and John 1:1–14. Passages such as John 3:35, 10:30, 14:10 and 17:3,11 were also central to the debate. Look through these passages and consider how you would respond to the Arian position.

The fourth-century church eventually concluded that Jesus' full divinity is necessary to humanity's eternal salvation. Arianism reduces Jesus to a creature, a created being, but only God can break the power of sin. Only the Eternal One can overcome sin for eternity (compare Hebrews 9:11–28). Salvation belongs to God and Jesus is Saviour.

Therefore we can say 'the one God is the trinity'; and not, 'in the one God there is the trinity'. All members of the Godhead are equally divine, even if their roles within the Godhead differ. One indivisible Godhead exists simultaneously in 3 different modes of being. In God's eternal form, outside the limits of space and time, God is eternally three.

Within this unity, Father, Son and Spirit have different functions; that is, their roles are functionally different. While the Son and Holy Spirit are equal to the Father in all of their attributes and divinity, they are subordinate to the Father in their roles. They are subordinate in office and operation, but not in essence, for the sake of humanity. This 'functional subordination' of Son and Spirit is relative to salvation history. In other words, God's redemption of humanity entails different divine roles but the differences in these roles are temporal, not eternal.

ACTIVITY

Can you think of examples of the distinct roles of Father, Son and Holy Spirit in human history?

The trinity works in unity: the entire trinity is involved in the actions of each member of the Godhead. In the words of the early church 'the external works of the trinity are undivided'. For instance, Father, Son and Spirit are all involved in creation. Yet, each member of the trinity also has a specific role in relation to humanity and the world. It is appropriate to think of:

- the Father as creator
- Christ as saviour
- the Spirit as sanctifier

Here we are affirming that creation is the work of the Father, redemption is the work of the Son and sanctification is the work of the Spirit. This idea is known as appropriation: each member of the Godhead has a primary responsibility appropriate to salvation while the entirety of salvation is the work of the one God.

Relationships and the Trinity

The centrality of relationship to the Godhead stands out as a hallmark of divinity. You recall that *persona* could best be understood as 'person in relationship'. The members of the trinity share in the lives of one another, in a mutual expression of love. As 1 John 4:8 asserts, 'God is love'. And in an astounding act of compassion, God extended his love to humanity. That love is the central ethic of the kingdom then should come as no surprise. God calls his people into a community founded on the sacrificial love that reflects his own love. To be God's people is to value relationship, just as God is a relational being.

ACTIVITY

If God is a God of relationship, and calls his people to be the same, what are the implications for your own life? And for the life of the church?

Ultimately, the limits of the human mind do not permit full comprehension of the trinity, as almost 2000 years of theological debate has proved. One of the ways that the early church dealt with the difficulty of understanding the trinity was to devise a number of symbols of it to express through images what words would not allow. A few of these are shown in Figure 1 below:

Figure 1

As Paul says of Christ: 'great is the mystery of godliness' (1 Timothy 3:16). Here he is referring to the incarnation, but the mystery can easily be extended to the trinity. Nonetheless, being able to express your own understanding of the Godhead is important to your own faith as well as for your witness to others.

ACTIVITY

How might you communicate your understanding of the trinity to a particular group of people (specify a group)? What image or story might you use?

UNIT II—THE CHRISTIAN LIFE

I have been crucified with
Christ,
and it is no longer I who live,
but it is Christ who lives in
me.
And the life I now live in the flesh
I live by faith in the Son of God,
who loved me and gave
himself for me.

Galatians 2:19b-20

Our study of God leads us to ask: how should we live in view of this creator, saviour and sanctifier of humanity? What does life in relationship to the trinitarian God look like?

In this unit, you will think about the Christian life, including what it means to be made in God's image, the impact of sin, the centrality of salvation, the importance of the church, and the practice of faith.

STUDIES

5 What is a Christian?

6 Salvation

7 Being the Church

8 Practicing Faith

What is a Christian?

Our goal in this study is to ask: what is a Christian? This question helps us to think through our identity as believers and to understand our role as God's people.

Bible Passages: Genesis 1:26–31 and Ephesians 2:1–10

STUDY QUESTIONS

What do we learn from the Genesis passage about God's purposes in creating humanity?

> ➤ In vv.26–27, who is humanity modelled after?
> ➤ How does humanity being created both male and female contribute to that model?
> ➤ What responsibilities does God give to humanity?

What does the Ephesians passage tell you about being a Christian?

> ➤ What is the state of humanity before receiving grace? (vv.1–3)
> ➤ What does God do for humanity and why? (vv.4–8)
> ➤ What are the consequences for Christians? (vv.5–6, 10)

Created in God's Image

To answer the question 'what is a Christian?' we will first consider what it means to be human.

ACTIVITY

What does it mean to be human?

An obvious response to this, based on the Genesis passage above, is that we are created beings. As the Genesis account makes clear, human beings and the rest of creation have something important in common. Like the sun, the moon, the dandelions and the squirrels, we are a part of God's created order. Our physicality affirms this. We are material beings who lead an embodied existence. In many ways, we are our bodies, and, as we will discuss in Study 6, redemption involves our physical bodies.

Consequently, human beings find expression as well as self-understanding through their cultural and historical context. We gain self-definition through not only the place where we live but also the period of history in which we live. This goes below the surface of clothing and hairstyles, down to the very heart of how people perceive themselves, their lives and their world.

Within the Christian understanding, human beings are identified in relation to God. Even those who have no belief in God are nonetheless his creations. We are not autonomous individuals, free to govern our own existence independent of any divine being or even the people around us. The freedom we do experience comes from being made in God's image.

The phrase 'image of God' (which is often written in Latin: the *imago Dei*) derives from the story of the creation of humanity. The final, crowning act of creation in Genesis 1 is the forming of a being in God's own likeness. Human beings are the high-point of creation, because we are made in God's image. It is this image that makes us different from the rest of creation. In some finite way, we reflect God. This image gives us dignity and value, and it is the source of human rights and responsibilities.

Being made in God's image gives us a connection to God. We can address God and respond to him; in short, we can have a relationship with him. Unlike other animals, humans are able to rise above the demands of our own immediate needs and engage with the world from God's eye view. We live with a dynamic sense of moving forwards, towards the future, and towards the Eternal One.

Man is one of your creatures, Lord, and his instinct is to praise you.

He bears about him the mark of death, the sign of his own sin, to remind him that you thwart the proud. But still, since he is part of your creation, he wishes to praise you. The thought of you stirs so deeply that he cannot be content unless he praises you, because you made us for yourself and our hearts find no peace until they rest in you.

Augustine (354-430)

If we are made in God's image, then, in what way do we reflect God? How do we function as mirrors of our Creator?

ACTIVITY

What is the nature of this image? How do you think we reflect God?

This question has a variety of potential answers. Some assert that we reflect God through our physical form. In the incarnation, Jesus takes on human form, somehow introducing human physicality into the Godhead. Yet our physical resemblance to Jesus is due not to God being human in form, but due to God becoming flesh (John 1:14), an act of humility and self-emptying on Jesus' part (Philippians 2:6–7).

Others assert that our reflection of God resides in our ability to think and reason. Our capacity to think mirrors the wisdom and intelligence of God. But there is a danger here: limiting the image of God to human reason underestimates the importance of human emotion and physicality.

Alternatively, our free will could be said to be the chief component of this image. Human beings make decisions and exercise choice. We are creative, like our Creator, willing new things into existence, whether a piano concerto, computer technology or a new line of clothing.

The image of God is also a matter of function. After creating humanity, God tells them to 'have dominion' over the earth, giving them responsibility for his brand new creation (Genesis 1:26). Dominion is about stewardship. Humanity does not own creation—God does—but humanity is called upon to care for the world. This responsibility includes power over other creatures, a power that reflects God's own power to create, nurture and guide.

ACTIVITY

If God has given us responsibility for the created order, how ought we to treat it? Think of examples locally, nationally, internationally. How has humanity abused such responsibility?

Finally, it can be said that to be made in God's image is to be relational. This explanation of the image of God directly reflects the nature of the trinity. As you saw in Study 4, God is three-in-one, a community of being. To reflect the essential nature of God, we must be in relationship. The co-existence of male and female, from the very beginning of human creation (Genesis 1:27), is an expression of the relational nature of humanity. We find our identity through our co-existence with other people, as well as other creatures.

In New Testament terms, the ultimate expression of God's image is to be found in Jesus.

ACTIVITY

Read 2 Corinthians 4:4 and Colossians 1:15 for descriptions of Jesus as the image of God. See also Romans 5:12–21 for Paul's description of Jesus as the new Adam, the new beginning for humanity.

Jesus is the perfect reflection of God. He provides us with a model for life, for in his humanity he exemplifies what God intended all of humanity to be.

Fallen Beings

Sin disfigures the image of God in humanity. The human mirror is cracked, providing but a poor reflection ('image') of God. To understand the human condition, it is important to take sin into account.

ACTIVITY

How would you define sin: what is it? What are its effects? You may find it useful to read Mark 7:14–23.

Thinking about what sin does helps you to understand what it is. Sin involves 'doing wrong'; it is a corruption of the good. Sin counters the good of God's creation and is evident through the damage it causes. The good comes first—as seen in the passage at the beginning of this study—and sin can exist only as a distortion of this good. A useful analogy is to think of sin as the rust on a bicycle. The rust corrodes and will eventually ruin your bike, but it would not be an issue if you did not have a bike in the first place.

Sin, however, runs deeper than conduct. It is more than transgression of a moral code. You have already seen that human beings were created for relationship. Sin distorts those relationships, not only with each other and with God but also with our selves, our bodies and all of creation. This is because sin can be understood as a state of being: our will is in bondage to evil. Our 'wrong conduct' is a product of our internal disorientation, which leads to us preferring or desiring evil. The New Testament describes sin as a power that enslaves us (Romans 7). Humans are unable to break free from this power, either as individuals or in our organizational and societal structures.

Augustine likened sin to a spiritual illness that affects the whole of humanity. Sometimes the name 'original sin' is used to indicate that humanity as a whole has inherited sin (from our first 'parents', Adam and Eve) so that all human beings are born with a sinful disposition. Most parents expend huge amounts of energy teaching their children to behave, but very few have to teach their children how to misbehave!

ACTIVITY

Read Romans 7:7–25 for Paul's description of the human will's battle with sin. Do you identify with this passage in any way?

Vessels of Grace, Bearers of Faith

God's cure for sin is grace. Grace may be defined as God's unmerited attention to his fallen world. It encapsulates how God acts towards his creation, and it has a universal dimension. But it also has a personal side: grace is the assistance that God gives to humanity, even though we do not deserve it. As Ephesians 2 indicates, God's assistance is freely given, not earned. The supreme manifestation of grace is God sending his Son into the world to die for humanity.

What does grace do? God's assistance in our lives is generous and active. Through grace, God seeks to restore us to himself. Grace confronts the sinner, liberating us from our bondage to sin. It enables faith in Christ and empowers us to choose good, restoring us to relationship with God and his people. Grace heals human sinfulness by transforming human nature, reversing the disfigurement of sin.

ACTIVITY

Can you point to an act of grace in your life?

The human response to grace is faith. A well-known definition of faith is found in Hebrews 11:1: 'Faith is the assurance of things hoped for, the conviction of things not seen'. But what does this mean? Faith involves trust. The Christian responds to God's gracious attention by trusting him. People place their faith in all sorts of things—money, education, the news, science, favourite celebrities, their physician. The question is: in whom, or what, do you put your trust to guide you through life?

In the Old Testament, faith involves obedience as well as trust and intellectual assent. The Hebrew word for faith (*emunah*, like the related word *amen*) points to God's constancy, and Israel is called to trust in the truth of God's promises (Deuteronomy 30:1–20). The New Testament applies this idea to Christ. Faith places the whole life of the believer under Christ's Lordship. A trinitarian definition would be: faith is trust in the God revealed in Christ through the Holy Spirit.

ACTIVITY

Faith and belief are often linked together. Are they the same thing? If not, how do they differ?

Belief and faith, while both important, cannot be equated. To believe in something is not the same as putting your trust in it. Belief can be described as an intellectual assent to a set of doctrines or to an ideological system. Those who believe in God may acknowledge that he exists, without ever trusting him.

Martin Luther described faith using the image of a ship. Standing on dry land and asserting that you believe a particular ship will safely take you to the other side of the sea is not an act of faith. Getting on the ship and embarking upon a voyage shows trust. The ship must prove reliable to justify this faith. In the same way, a believer's faith in God's promises is effective because of the greatness of God.

While faith incorporates belief, it goes beyond and is greater than belief. Is faith, then, a leap away from reason into an unknown, intellectual darkness?

It is not possible either to empirically prove or disprove the existence of God. Science can access the material world only, and faith in God takes the believer beyond the realm of empirical knowledge. In this way, faith goes beyond reason. Yet faith and reason also work together, for faith is not blind trust but has to do with what you think. Faith is built upon belief and understanding, both of which utilise your ability to reason. The medieval theologian Anselm of Canterbury (1033–1109) described this as 'faith seeking understanding': faith that endeavours to make sense of the world.

The doctrine of justification by faith was at the heart of the sixteenth-century Protestant reformation. It asserts that faith is essential to salvation. Such faith has a personal reference: it is trust in the person and saving work of Jesus Christ, establishing the believer in a relationship with their Saviour. Faith is not just historical knowledge about Jesus' existence; faith is built upon trust in God's promises. And this faith comes from God himself, and is itself a product of grace.

ACTIVITY

Faith and works are sometimes viewed in opposition. Compare Galatians 2:15–21 to James 2:14–26. How is it that works 'complete' faith?

Being a Disciple

The person who has faith in Jesus is his disciple. Disciple means 'follower' and implies being a learner. Christians are people who follow Christ and learn from him (see Mark 1:16–18). Following encompasses your whole life, including direction and purpose. It also means modelling your life upon Christ. Discipleship is about how we live as Christians, and it involves on-going transformation.

The life of a disciple has Christ at its centre. Not church activities, not worship, not social justice, not theology, not even the Bible, not even the church itself. Just Jesus. All of these other things are important to the life of a Christian, but they must flow out of a focus upon Jesus as Lord. It is important to ask: how are you living? Who or what motivates your life? Who you are and how you live directly affect your relationship with God.

ACTIVITY

Complete the following sentences:

'I am a Christian because...'

'What I find most appealing about Jesus is...'

'Three ways I express my faith include...'

What then is a Christian? Being God's creation, bearing the image of God, wrestling with a sinful nature, receiving grace and responding with faith are all key in the life of a disciple. These components are brought together in salvation, which you will look at in the next study. At the heart of being a Christian is following Jesus.

Salvation

The source of the Christian life is salvation in Christ. To be a Christian is to have Christ's salvation. In this study, you will think about what salvation means as understood through the cross and the resurrection of Christ.

Bible Passages: John 12:20–36 and 1 Corinthians 15:12–28

STUDY QUESTIONS

Using the John passage, what did Jesus believe about his death?

➤ What is the value of the death of a single grain, and how is this related to servanthood? (vv.23–26)

➤ What does Jesus' death accomplish?

➤ The phrase 'lifted up' refers to Jesus being lifted up on the cross for all to see. What is the result, and how is it related to light?

What does the Corinthians' passage tell you about the necessity of the resurrection?

➤ What did the Corinthians believe about the resurrection? (v.12)

➤ What are the results of their misconception? (vv.13–19)

➤ What are the actual consequences of the resurrection, and, in particular, what enemy does the resurrection defeat? (vv.20–26)

Introducing Salvation

The biblical idea of salvation entails deliverance or liberation, particularly from danger, captivity or death. Salvation sets people free from the power of sin and death, through faith in Christ's act of redemption, restored by grace to a relationship with God. The groundwork for this is laid out in the Old Testament 'exodus' event, in which a multitude of slaves are miraculously delivered from their oppressor through divine intervention, symbolically protected from death by blood, and formed into a nation in covenant to the living all-powerful God.

In the New Testament, salvation refers not only to a past event but also to an ongoing process that is consummated in the future kingdom. Your salvation renews the image of God within you, moving you forward towards your final destiny when you will be eternally with and like Christ. To talk about salvation is to talk about Christ, for salvation is grounded in his life, death and resurrection. For the remainder of this study, we will concentrate upon the meaning of the cross and the resurrection.

The Work of the Cross

The cross is at the heart of salvation. Jesus' death on the cross achieves something that establishes a new situation in history, reversing the ultimate effect of evil in the world. The doctrine of the work of Christ on the cross is referred to as the atonement. Atonement means, quite literally 'at-one-ment', pointing to the reconciliation of humanity to God.

Paul asserts in 1 Corinthians 15:3, 'Christ died for our sins in accordance with the Scriptures' (the 'Scriptures' here refer to the Old Testament, since the New Testament was still in the making). What then is the relationship between Jesus' death and the forgiveness of sins? How does the cross enable salvation?

Scripture uses a number of terms and ideas to convey the work of the cross. Some of these have been developed as 'theories of the atonement', providing an explanation for how the cross atones for sins. It is perhaps useful to think of these as windows that provide a particular view onto the contents of the house that is the cross. While these views do not all link neatly together, they are also not mutually exclusive. Together they provide a fuller picture of what was achieved at the cross. We will look at four views here.

1ST VIEW: SACRIFICE

ACTIVITY

Read Hebrews 8:1 –10:18. According to this passage, how does Israelite practice foreshadow Jesus? What is the relationship between the old covenant and the new one in Christ? How does each covenant deal with sin?

The New Testament presents Jesus' death as a sacrifice on behalf of humanity, based on the Old Testament notion of sacrifice. To live with a holy God, the Israelites needed a method for dealing with their sin. This is described in the Jewish sacrificial system, where sin is dealt with by the offering of sacrifice. At the ordination of Aaron and his sons, bulls are offered 'as a sin offering for atonement' for the new priests (Exodus 29:31–36). Sin offerings function as atoning sacrifices, not only for individuals but also for the whole community (Leviticus 1:4, 4:13–21). One day per year in the Jewish calendar—Yom Kippur—is set aside as the Day of Atonement. The purpose of this day is 'to cleanse you; from all your sins you shall be clean before the LORD' (Leviticus 16:30).

Building upon Old Testament imagery and practice, the book of Hebrews depicts the cross as the ultimate and conclusive act of sacrifice. Old Testament sacrifice foreshadows, and indeed is fulfilled in the sacrifice of Jesus on the cross. Jesus is both the innocent victim, the lamb who is slain (1 Peter 1:19), and the priest who offers the sacrifice (Ephesians 5:2). At the very beginning of Jesus' ministry, John the Baptist describes him as 'the Lamb of God who takes away the sin of the world' (John 1:29). Jesus is sent into the world to die for humanity.

Unlike the sacrifices of the Old Testament, Jesus' sacrifice occurs once, is perfect and counts for eternity (Hebrews 7:27). The incarnation is key here, for both Jesus' humanity and divinity are necessary to make the sacrifice effective. As you saw at the end of Study 2, humanity's full salvation is dependent upon Jesus' humanity. Jesus must be fully human for his salvation to permeate every aspect of human existence. As our priestly mediator, Jesus sacrifices himself and because he is divine, his sacrifice has eternal results.

2ND VIEW: SUBSTITUTION

ACTIVITY

Read Isaiah 53:2–12 and Romans 3:21–26. In the Isaiah passage, what burden does Jesus bear in his death? Why does he die and what is the result for humanity? According to the Romans passage, why does God present Jesus as a sacrifice? How are believers made righteous?

Jesus takes our place in his death. As Israel's representative, the Messiah stands in the place of Israel and all of humanity. The idea of Jesus as our substitute finds meaning in the context of Old Testament sacrifice, which we discussed above. But the New Testament also couples substitution with the idea of justification.

Justification draws upon a legal metaphor. A righteous and just God created humanity 'good', to be in eternal fellowship with him. Human disobedience erects a barrier between God and humanity. Should God simply 'overlook' this barrier? It is hard to see how this would be a just and right response. God does not say that evil may be 'overlooked', rather that it must be punished and eradicated. In this way God will act justly in the face of the many terrible things we find in our world: murder, rape, torture, genocide ... the last century has made this list longer than ever.

However since, as Paul says, all people sin, all should be condemned and should, on this understanding, be put to death—removed from God's presence (Romans 6:23). Acquittal depends upon a change of legal status before God. Humanity has neither the resources to pay the penalty for sin, nor the strength to break free from its power. The change of status occurs through the death of Christ, who does have the resources: since he is divine, the worth of his death is eternal. Due to his humanity, his death counts for the human race.

God condemns sin and the location of that condemnation is in Jesus' human flesh (Romans 8:3). Romans 3:25 calls Jesus the 'place of atonement' (or 'reconciliation'). The Greek word used here may be translated to emphasize both the removal of God's anger by offering a gift, and the removal of human guilt. Christ dies in place of guilty humanity, appeasing God's wrath towards sin.

On the cross, therefore, Jesus is humanity's substitute (1 Timothy 2:5–6 and 1 Peter 2:24). The judgement that believers receive from God is justification rather than condemnation; we are pronounced not guilty, forgiven, set free from slavery to sin, and we receive righteousness through faith. Justification leads to life (Romans 4:25 and 5:18).

> *My sin—O the joy of this*
> *glorious thought*
> *My sin, not in part, but the*
> *whole,*
> *Is nailed to the cross,*
> *and I bear it no more:*
> *Praise the Lord, Praise the*
> *Lord,*
> *O my soul!*
>
> Philip P. Bliss[1]

---

[1] From the hymn 'It is Well with My Soul'

3RD VIEW: RECONCILIATION

ACTIVITY

Read John 3:11–21 and 2 Corinthians 5:16–21. According to these passages, why did God send his Son to the cross? What responses does Jesus' death evoke? What does it mean to be reconciled to God?

A superficial view of the atonement could lead you to view God as an angry deity who wants to punish all those who transgress his moral law. But Scripture will not allow this. Another angle on the atonement emphasizes God's love, and the relationship with humanity that God longs for.

The New Testament develops this idea using a relationship metaphor: reconciliation. Through the cross, Jesus acts as an agent of reconciliation between humanity and God. God forgives humanity and we can once more enter his presence. The result is what Paul calls 'adoption': the Father adopts Christians into his family (Galatians 4:4–7). As God's children, we receive inheritance rights alongside of Jesus (Romans 8:15–17).

Some proponents of this view of the atonement stress the subjective impact of the cross upon the believer: the 'moral influence' of Jesus' example. When believers look at the cross, they see God's love and respond to it with love. The atonement finds its fruition in the transformation of the believer's life.

4TH VIEW: VICTORY

ACTIVITY

Read Hebrews 2:14–18 and Colossians 2:13–15. Based on these passages, what did Jesus' death accomplish? Whom did the cross defeat? What are the results for believers?

Our study so far may lead you to think that the work of the cross is aimed solely at humanity. But Scripture does not permit such a narrow interpretation. The passages above portray Jesus' death as a victory over the forces of evil, a view called the *Christus Victor* (Christ the Victor) theory of the atonement. The Messiah overcomes the evil introduced into God's world, back in Genesis 3, by defeating the powers that have corrupted creation—sin, death and Satan (see 1 Corinthians 15:54–57).

The cross is the turning point in a cosmic conflict between God and evil. Christ is God's champion and the cross his battle of victory over sin. On the cross, God offers Jesus as a ransom for sinners. Ransom is a technical term referring to the purchase or liberation of a slave or war prisoner. Everyone who sins 'is a slave to sin' (John 8:24–26). Jesus' death liberates sinners from sin to serve him as their Lord.

Christ defeats sin with its own weapon: death. Satan seizes Jesus in death, but can't keep him there. The devil, who has the power of death, is disarmed. Humanity is redeemed. The word redemption is rooted in the idea of a business transaction and is often used as a synonym for salvation. To redeem something is to buy it back, even at a costly price. Jesus secures humanity's release from bondage to sin by paying the ultimate price: death.

ACTIVITY

Take some time to review the four views of the atonement described here. How does each one contribute towards your understanding of the work of Jesus on the cross? Can you think of any hymns or stories that illustrate these ideas?

It is not necessary to narrow our understanding of the atonement down to one view. The sixteenth-century reformer, John Calvin (1509–64), described Jesus' ministry as a threefold office: prophet, priest and king. These three 'offices' or roles provide a model for drawing together various views of the atonement.

As a prophet, Jesus taught about God's kingdom, giving instructions to his disciples on how to live in light of that kingdom. The view of the atonement that stresses the need to respond to God's love is relevant here. In his role as priest, Jesus dies for humanity, drawing upon both the sacrifice and substitution views of the atonement. Finally, as king, Jesus conquers evil through the cross, establishes his Lordship, and promises the ultimate victory of God in the world. This office, of course, points to the victory model of the atonement.

The Resurrection

Salvation is not, however, dependent solely upon the cross. The resurrection is also crucial. Paul asserts in 1 Corinthians 15:17, 'if Christ has not been raised, your faith is futile; you are still in your sins.' Without the resurrection, the atonement doesn't work. Christ's death was not enough to effect salvation; he also had to be raised to life. Why is this?

ACTIVITY

Why do you think Christ's resurrection is important? What do you believe about the resurrection of believers?

The Corinthian church seems to have asked similar questions to the ones we are posing here, and you have already looked at the passage where Paul answers them (in 1 Corinthians 15). The Corinthians did not believe that the physical body is raised to life. They may have believed in a 'resurrection' (or at least a continuation) of a person's spirit after death, but not in a bodily resurrection. Paul responds by arguing for the necessity of the resurrection, in vv.1–34. The remainder of the chapter he devotes to a discussion of the nature of these resurrection bodies. We will look at that discussion in Study 21.

Paul first establishes, in vv.1–11, that the resurrection is central to the gospel message. Then in v.12, he states the Corinthian position. Next Paul asks: what happens if you Corinthians are right and there is no physical resurrection (vv.13–19)? Notice that the word 'if' dominates this passage. Paul shows his readers the logical conclusions of their position.

The primary consequence is stated in v.13: if a human body cannot be physically raised from the dead, then Christ was not raised. If resurrection as a general principle is not possible, then Jesus' resurrection as a specific instance was not possible. The result, as far as salvation is concerned, is found in vv.16–17. If Jesus passed out of the physical world into the world of the spirit, there is no release from sin, and our faith is in vain.

Paul's rebuttal comes in verse 20: Jesus has indeed been physically raised from the dead. In particular, the resurrection defeats death (v.26; see also v.55). Jesus does not just die like Lazarus (John 11), and return to life in the same state as he was in prior to death, only to die again later. Rather, Jesus goes through death and comes out the other side into eternal life, defeating death's power.

ACTIVITY

How is the defeat of death related to salvation?

Jesus' personal victory over death ensures the ultimate defeat of death for humanity. Paul describes Jesus' resurrection as the first fruit of a larger harvest (v.20): Jesus' resurrection both represents and guarantees the resurrection of all believers. It reverses the direction of humanity's current path. Whereas our ultimate destiny was death, now it is life.

The resurrection is thus essential to salvation because, otherwise, death still wins. If Christ was not physically raised from the dead, then his body would have remained in the tomb. Sin and death would still have Jesus' body in their grip, and therefore the fate of the created order would not have been altered (see also Romans 6:9–10). Without the resurrection, the gospel is rendered powerless to make any difference in the physical world. In the resurrection, God intervenes decisively in the world, defeating sin and death's power and providing a path to life that the entirety of the created order longs for (Romans 8:19–22).

ACTIVITY

In what ways would you say that death is still an enemy to humanity?

Death continues to cast a shadow over human life. Right now, we live in the age between the first fruit, Jesus' resurrection, and the final harvest. Death fills our newspapers, television screens and hospitals. Humanity cannot escape or defeat it, despite our best attempts through advances in medicine, science, hygiene and world-wide food distribution. The defeat of death through the resurrection is a message pertinent to all of God's created order.

Being the Church

As far as the New Testament is concerned, being a Christian means being a part of the church. Here you will consider what it means to be the church as you look at the nature of the church as it is portrayed in Scripture.

Bible Passage: 1 Corinthians 12:12–26

STUDY QUESTIONS

What do we learn from this passage about the church?

➢ Who is the church's source of unity? (vv.12–13,18)

➢ In vv.14–20, Paul stresses the need for diversity. What are the implications of this for the church?

➢ What would happen if every part of the body performed the same function?

➢ In vv.21–26, Paul highlights the interdependence between body members. What would happen if stronger body members rejected some of the less visible members?

➢ Imagery is best conveyed visually. Take a few moments to draw a picture or a series of pictures that visualize Paul's points about the church as a body.

What is the Church?

ACTIVITY

What comes to mind when you hear the word 'church'? How is the word commonly used?

If you asked a non-churchgoing friend to define 'church', no doubt their definition would refer to a building or a Sunday morning service. Others may expand the definition to include a denomination such as the Anglican Church. All of these definitions are correct in so far as they express the current usage of 'church'. However, the way the word is used in the Bible is different.

In Scripture, the church is always people: God's people in community. The New Testament refers to the church as the *ekklesia*, which means 'assembly' (the study of the church is called 'ecclesiology', a direct derivation of this word). *Ekklesia* was used for assemblies of people in general, and is occasionally used in the New Testament for an assembly other than the church. However, primarily, a church is an assembly of God's people. Jesus assembles together a people of God, for God.

What kind of assembly are we talking about? 'Church' is used in a variety of ways. In passages such as Acts 8:1, Romans 16:16 and 2 Thessalonians 1:4, it refers to a particular, local group of Christians who meet together in Christ's name. The idea of the local church is rooted in this theological understanding. The community of Christians in a particular location is church.

Yet the church is also universal. Passages such as Matthew 16:18, 1 Corinthians 15:9, Ephesians 5:25 and Colossians 1:18 use 'church' for the worldwide company of God's people. The term universal church refers to all of God's people throughout the world and through all of history. The church is not only local but also worldwide.

ACTIVITY

Take a moment to read through a few of the passages listed in the two paragraphs above.

Perhaps the question should not be 'what' but 'who' is the church? Two other terms, visible and invisible, supply a potential answer. The invisible church refers to the community of true believers. They are 'invisible' now in that no one will know who truly belongs to this community until the end of human history. True members of Christ's body are those who have an 'invisible' relationship with Christ. The 'visible' church is everyone who comprises the life of the church now, while non-believers can and will be part of the visible church community.

ACTIVITY

This description of the church derives from the parables of the weeds and the wheat in Matthew 13:24–30, vv.36–43, and of the net of fish in Matthew 13:47–50. How might these parables be understood to describe the visible and invisible church? Do you agree with this interpretation?

The fifth-century theologian Augustine called the church a mixed body of saints and sinners. The church is sinful not only because of the non-believers present within it, but also due to the fallen nature of Christians. Since even the invisible church consists of forgiven sinners, it will contain sin until Christ's return.

Another way of answering 'who is the church?' is to examine the New Testament terms used for believers.

ACTIVITY

Some of the New Testament terms referring to groups of believers include: brothers and sisters (or brothers) (1 Thessalonians 4:1); the disciples (Acts 6:7, 9:36); the saints (Philippians 1:1); Christians (Acts 11:26); and those belonging to the Way (Acts 9:2). What does each term tell us about the church?

Did you note that each of these terms has to do with people? When Paul writes to the church in Thessalonica, he foregrounds the family nature of the church by repeatedly calling the Thessalonians 'brothers' (a broad term encompassing both males and females; hence the translation 'brothers and sisters'). You will recall from Study 5 that a disciple refers to a personal follower of Christ. So, the church is comprised of Jesus' followers. The term 'saint' has a simple meaning in the New Testament: saints are those sanctified or 'set apart' by the Holy Spirit—in other words, all believers.

ACTIVITY

Does thinking of the church as people alter your own understanding of church in any way? If so, what are the implications?

The Church as God's Possession

While the church may be people, it is not just a group of individuals. Nor would it be correct to call any group or society 'church'. The church is a community of people who are in relation to the triune God. Put differently, the church may be defined as:

- a community in covenant to God,
- united by a shared faith in Christ,
- and given life by the Spirit.

This definition is deliberately trinitarian for the church belongs to God. The church is initiated by the Father, who 'reconciles us to himself through Christ' (2 Corinthians 5:18). This reconciliation effects a new humanity that exists in Christ: 'if anyone is in Christ, there is new creation' (2 Corinthians 5:17). The Holy Spirit transforms this new humanity into the image of Christ (2 Corinthians 3:18).

If the church belongs to God, how does it reflect this ownership? As Christ's body, the church has an organic relationship with God. As you saw in Study 4, the trinity is a living, divine fellowship. This divine fellowship provides the prototype for church community. The life of the church should be communal, reflecting the trinity, who is a community of being.

Christian communal life is two-directional. To be a member of Christ's body means to be related both to God *and* to the other members of the body. These two directions are often referred to as the Christian's vertical and horizontal relationships (see Figure 2). The vertical element ensures that the association of Christians is more than just a social gathering or club.

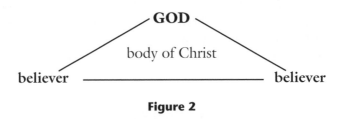

Figure 2

Being a disciple of Christ means belonging to the church. To be a member of Christ's body is to be connected to the other parts of that body. Being a lone ranger Christian is not an option. As Kevin Giles aptly puts it, 'the church is therefore not something extra in the Christian life, but the very essence of life in Christ.'[2]

We understand the *personae* of the trinity in terms of their relationships with one another. The Father is Father in respect to the Son, the Son is Son in respect to the Father, and the Spirit is the Spirit of God and of Christ. Similarly, people, made to reflect God's image, are fully human when they are in relationship. In Study 5, you saw that humanity is by nature communal. This community finds natural expression in the church. According to Paul, these relationships take precedence over individual rights or personal self-fulfilment.

ACTIVITY

Read Philippians 2:14 for an example of a passage where Paul calls upon Christians to pursue, not their own ends, but harmonious relationships with other Christians. How does this attitude differ from that of contemporary society?

In Study 4, you considered how the three members of the Godhead are all equally God, but have different roles to play. The church reflects this distinction in that all people are equal in Christ (Galatians 3:28) and yet each person has a distinct role to play in the body, depending upon their gifts.

ACTIVITY

Look at Galatians 3:26–29 and 1 Corinthians 12:4–6 (note that the latter verses are trinitarian). Based on these passages, why may the church be described as having unity in diversity?

Biblical Images of the Church

The Holy Spirit is at work in the world testifying to the gospel, and it is the church that is the primary channel for this testimony. The testimony occurs not only through verbal proclamation—evangelism—and service, but also through the building up of the church. In the church, God is gathering

---

[2] *What on Earth is the Church?* (London: SPCK, 1995) p.223

together a people for himself, an eschatological community that lives for God and his future kingdom. The church is not the kingdom, but rather, it anticipates and lives in preparation for the kingdom.

What images of the church do you find in Scripture? We have already repeatedly referred to the church as God's people. This phrase is rooted in the Old Testament declaration of Israel as God's people (Exodus 19:5, Leviticus 26:12). The New Testament in turn calls the church the 'Israel of God' (Galatians 6:16), continuing yet also re-shaping this idea. Israel's relationship with God was rooted in its covenant with Yhwh. Likewise, the church's relationship with God is rooted in the new covenant made in Jesus (Luke 22:20, Hebrews 9:15).

ACTIVITY

1 Peter 2:9–10 describes the church as a people belonging to God, or 'a people for God's possession'. According to these verses, how does God want the church to respond?

You began this study by thinking about the church as the body of Christ. This is an organic image, foregrounding life and unity. Christ is the head of this body, as well as its life source. Also prominent in New Testament imagery is the church as the bride of Christ (Ephesians 5:23–32, Revelation 19:7–9). Here Christ is the husband and the church's destiny is to be his bride. This image is future-oriented, calling the church to commitment and devotion as it prepares for its wedding day.

The church is also described as the building of God (1 Corinthians 3:10–17, Ephesians 2:19–22, 1 Peter 2:5). Within the Old Testament, the temple represents God's presence among his people. Under the new covenant, this temple is people (see 1 Corinthians 3:16–17, noting that the 'you' in these verses is plural). God the Holy Spirit now dwells within people, the community whose life is built on Christ. Another important image is the church as the family of God (Galatians 3:26–4:7, Romans 8:14–17). Paul calls the church the household of God (Ephesians 2:19, 1 Timothy 3:15), the place where God's family lives. A final significant image is the church as the flock of God. Jesus is the shepherd over this flock (John 10:1–30, 1 Peter 5:1–4).

> ## *ACTIVITY*
>
> What does each of these metaphors tell you about the church? If you are working in a group, have each person, or pairs of people, look at one metaphor. If you are working alone, choose one or two metaphors to investigate further.

Characteristics of the Church

In Study 4, you looked at the Nicene Creed, which was devised by the early church to articulate what it believed. This creed includes a statement about the church.

- We believe in one holy catholic and apostolic church.

The four adjectives used here, 'one, holy, catholic and apostolic', have been called the four marks of the church. These marks do not form a comprehensive doctrine of the church, but are rather a summary of its nature.

The assertion that the church should be 'one' is an assertion about unity. Scripture repeatedly calls the church to unity, a unity grounded in the trinitarian God (Ephesians 4:1–6). This unity, then, is theological, not sociological: unity and uniformity are not the same thing. Referring back to your study of the body imagery in 1 Corinthians 12, the church is called to maintain unity in diversity. Christians are not all meant to be the same, but all are meant to contribute to the edification of the body, that is, to one another.

> ## *ACTIVITY*
>
> Take a moment to read Ephesians 4:1–6. How do the fruit of the Spirit listed here contribute to unity?

Of course one of the most obvious characteristics of the worldwide church is that it is disunited at an institutional level. In part, this disunity is a natural result of the church's need to adapt to its context. Adapting to local culture leads to local churches, and these local churches will invariably be culturally diverse. However, some of the disunity stems from failure to prioritize the unity of the body over less central issues and is a matter for repentance.

The second mark calls the church to be 'holy', that is, to be separated out as God's. The church is set apart from the world by God, to serve God by being God's people. The aim of this separation is not to be different from the world, but to belong to God. While this separation may—and indeed does—have moral implications, it is grounded in relationship to God. Holiness of lifestyle is a function of relationship to God, and not the other way around. You do not have to live in a certain way in order to be a Christian, but being in relationship with God will motivate you to live in a way that honours God.

ACTIVITY

A friend asserts 'I could never be good enough to be a Christian'. How might you respond?

Next, the church is called 'catholic' (with a small 'c'). The word catholic means universal and, as you saw above, refers to all of the people of God in the world at any time. Each local church represents the universal church of which it is a part. No one is rejected, and the church can be found wherever there are two or three believers gathered in Jesus' name (Matthew 18:20).

Finally, the church is described as 'apostolic'. This mark has two implications. It gives the church historical roots: the church was built upon Jesus' initial followers who bore witness to the gospel (Ephesians 2:20) and has historical continuity with them. It also gives the church direction. To be apostolic is to continue the work of the apostles. The church carries on in mission, teaching and leadership, following the tradition of the apostles.

Practicing Faith

If you have worked your way through all of the studies so far, you will know that your faith is intended to permeate every aspect of your existence. Christianity is about who you are, and what you do is a function of who you are. The practice of the Christian faith can take numerous forms, depending upon the individual, their church and its context. Yet there are certain important practices that most believers have in common. Here we will think about worship, including prayer, fellowship, ministry and the sacraments.

Bible passage: Colossians 3:1–17

STUDY QUESTIONS

What do you learn from this passage about life as a Christian?

➢ What does it mean to seek 'things that are above' and not earthly things? (vv.1–3)

➢ Some of these earthly things are listed in vv.5–9. Why should you rid your life of these?

➢ In vv.9b,10, Paul uses a clothing metaphor to describe the alteration in the Christian life. How has the Christian changed, and what is happening to the new self?

➢ What new clothing does Paul want the Christian to seek actively (compare v.1) and to put on? (vv.12–17)

➢ Paul is talking not just to the individual, but to the whole church. How does each item you named above contribute to the life and well-being of the church?

Worship

The New Testament uses two words for worship that help to clarify its nature. The first of these, *proskuneō* (literally, 'to kiss towards'), evokes an image of bowing in humility and love before God. This is a deliberate, specific act. To worship God is to come before him in adoration, expressing the praise and love that are his due as our Creator and Saviour. Similarly, one of the original meanings of the English word 'worship' was 'worth-ship': reflecting the worth of the thing or person worshipped.

The other New Testament word for worship is *latreuō*, meaning 'to serve'. Worship is the service that believers render to God. The phrase 'worship service' has its roots here, although the word has the broader meaning of worship as a lifestyle. Thus, you may view your whole life as worship.

A useful analogy that draws these two together is to think of worship as an expression of love. Washing your children's clothes or earning money to pay for their piano lessons enacts love through service. However, it is also important to say 'I love you' or to give your children a hug—acts that overtly express your love. Likewise, our worship of God finds expression both through specific acts and daily lifestyle.

ACTIVITY

How do you worship God?

The focus of worship for Christians is God. Our studies in Unit I portray a God who deserves worship. We worship God because of who he is and what he does. What God does includes his acts, not only in history and the world but also in our personal life, as well as his promises for the future. As we worship, we are exposed to this living, active God.

We worship God because we are in relationship with him. We meet with God because of God taking the initiative: worship is empowered by the Holy Spirit (Philippians 3:3). We respond to God in worship, as well as express to him our thoughts, gratitude and concerns. We can come to him no matter how we feel. It is an effort of will to focus on God, more than a question of feelings.

The Psalms provide a model of coming before God in every imaginable emotional state. Psalm 103, for instance, is an expression of personal trust in God, while Psalm 51 confesses sin. Psalm 42 communicates grief and Psalm 88 struggles with despair, while Psalm 96 shouts praise.

ACTIVITY

Read through the Psalms listed above, noticing how they include questions, praise, thanksgiving and even anger. Write your own Psalm. Use it to express your own feelings or situation to God.

Worship is not only personal but also corporate. The whole body of Christ is called to worship God. As the temple of the Holy Spirit (1 Corinthians 3:16), the church is the locus of praise to God. To use an analogy, just as the human body is strengthened through exercise that incorporates a variety of muscles and body organs, so the body of Christ is strengthened through spiritual exercise that enables it to function as a unit. Acts of worship and service strengthen the church.

ACTIVITY

Read 1 Corinthians 14:26. Here, Paul is describing the worship of the Corinthian church. What is his guiding principle?

'Let all things be done for building up' is Paul's rule of thumb. Although the focus of worship is God, its practice should edify the corporate body. While you sing a song of praise to Jesus, the singing should occur in a way that enables everyone present to worship. Some songs specifically address fellow worshippers, encouraging mutual worship of God.

Worship is, of course, one of the most distinguishing features of contemporary local churches. Many people choose their church based on its worship style. How a church structures its worship says a good deal about what the church believes is important in its relationship with God. A significant element in this worship is often music. Worship and singing cannot be equated, yet music is a powerful form of communication.

ACTIVITY

What does the structure and contents of your church's worship services say about its view of God?

Prayer

An important part of worship is prayer. If God is with you all the time, then prayer is about responding to and communicating with him. Setting aside time to talk to God develops your relationship with him. Even Jesus, who knew God's constant presence, withdrew to pray (Mark 1:35). Imagine spending a day with a good friend but never speaking to them, or only speaking if you have a request to make. What impact might this have upon your relationship?

Living the Christian life means entering a two-way dialogue with God. And dialogue involves both speaking and listening. Unfortunately, we frequently reduce prayer to 'intercession', that is, to making requests. The danger is that we turn prayer into something we do. Prayer in the Bible is usually a response to who God is, and then, sometimes, a request for God to act.

ACTIVITY

Read Daniel 9:1–19 for Daniel's prayer for the Jewish people and Jerusalem. What does Daniel's prayer incorporate besides intercession?

Daniel confesses his people's sins, in light of who God is. His prayer is a response, not only to the words of a prophecy (v.3) but also to God's character. Confession is an important part of prayer, as are thanksgiving and praise.

Perhaps the best-known example of biblical prayer is the Lord's Prayer. Unlike many other biblical prayers, it is unusual because it doesn't arise out of a particular struggle or difficulty. It is simply given to the disciples as a model of how to pray.

ACTIVITY

What kind of model does the Lord's Prayer provide? Examine Matthew 6:9–13 and see whether you find in it elements of praise, thanksgiving, intercession, or confession.

We are not on our own in prayer. The Holy Spirit enables us to pray, guiding us in our encounter with the living God (Romans 8:26–27). Prayer then is not about fulfilling needs but about getting to know God better, as you yield to his Spirit at work within you.

Fellowship

The relationship that believers have with one another is described in Scripture as *koinōnia:* communion or fellowship. Fellowship expresses community and is a significant part of the Spirit-inspired Christian life.

Fellowship is generated by believers' common participation in the life of God. The glue binding fellowship together is self-sacrificial love for others, the type of love that Jesus models in his death (Colossians 3:14, 1 John 3:16). This fellowship has numerous points of expression. Among these are:

- hospitality (1 Peter 4:9)
- mutual encouragement (Hebrews 10:25)
- support (Galatians 6:2)
- prayer for one another (Colossians 4:2–4)
- forgiveness (Colossians 3:13)

As we will discuss later, the Eucharist is a particular expression of fellowship.

ACTIVITY

At the end of a number of his letters, Paul includes an ethical or practical section exhorting believers in their relationships with each other. Refer to your study of Colossians 3:1–17 for an example. How does this enable fellowship?

Ministry and Spiritual Gifts

Ministry is service of God for the benefit of other people. The New Testament word for service, *diakonia,* is used at times to refer to specialized ministries within the church, such as elders, bishops and deacons (who are, quite literally, servants). Ministry can thus be a form of church vocation. But the word also has broader scope, recognizing as ministry any service for, in or by the church.

All church members have spiritual gifts and the exercise of many of these gifts is ministry. Spiritual gifts, in fact, enable a person to serve the church. The Greek word for gift in most of the relevant biblical passages is *charisma,* or gift of grace. These gifts make the work of the Spirit evident and are given by Jesus to enable his body to serve him, each other, and the world for the gospel. Ministry therefore is an expression of the work of the Holy Spirit in the church.

Some spiritual gifts, such as healing, provide obvious manifestations of the Spirit at work. Other gifts, such as administration, clearly dovetail with an individual's natural talents and abilities; yet these gifts are also evidence of the Spirit at work in the life of the individual and the church.

ACTIVITY

Take a few minutes to examine 1 Corinthians 12:4–7. What three labels does Paul use for the gifts? What insight does each label provide? Why does God give gifts?

Romans 12:6–8, 1 Corinthians 12:8–10,28–30, Ephesians 4:11 and 1 Peter 4:11 contain the main New Testament lists of spiritual gifts. Comparing them will show you that none of these lists are intended to be comprehensive; rather, they are all representative of the types of gifts bestowed by the Spirit. Discovering and exercising your personal gifts is an important part of being a member of Christ's body. When you exercise your gifts, for the good of the body, the whole body benefits. Paul encourages not only exercising your gifts, but also striving for new ones (1 Corinthians 14:1).

ACTIVITY

A good way to explore your gifts is to discuss them with other Christians. If you are working in a group, spend some time discussing each other's gifts. This should include not only what each person is good at, but also what each person enjoys, in their service of the church. If you are working alone, take time out to discuss this with another Christian who knows you well.

The Sacraments

An important part of the Christian life is participation in the sacraments Jesus gave his church. Although the number of sacraments recognized by various church traditions is variable, there are two, baptism and the Eucharist, which are recognized by all church traditions.

The word 'sacrament' means 'sign'. The sacraments function theologically as a sign of God's grace, or, as Augustine put it, 'an outward and visible sign of an inward and invisible grace'. The 'visible sign' refers to the physical aspect of the sacrament, while the 'invisible grace' refers to the spiritual reality that accompanies the sacrament.

The relationship between the sign and grace is interpreted in a variety of ways, and it is here that the various church traditions particularly differ. It is perhaps easiest to think of the differences as existing along a spectrum. At one end of the spectrum is the belief that the sign enacts but doesn't bestow grace. Baptism, on this view, demonstrates that a believer belongs to the church. The emphasis rests with the believer's acceptance of the promise that accompanies the sign. Baptism is effective when the believer receives baptism by faith and joins the church community.

At the other end of the spectrum is the belief that the sign both enacts and bestows grace. In other words, the sign in some way conveys God's grace to believers. Here, baptism not only demonstrates that a person belongs to the church, but also bestows a grace that enables that belonging. On this view, the sacraments are effective in themselves. While there are church traditions that occupy one end or the other of this spectrum, many others fall somewhere in the middle.

ACTIVITY

Where does your church fall in this range of views? How has this influenced your participation in the sacraments?

The Eucharist—or, if you prefer, the Lord's Supper, Communion, the Breaking of Bread, Mass or the Divine Liturgy—was instituted by Jesus at the Last Supper and is rooted in the Jewish Passover. It draws together the past, present and future of salvation, with the aim of sustaining and sharing in the Christian life.

The meaning of the Eucharist operates on multiple levels, all within the context of salvation. A useful way to remember its significance is to think of arrows pointing in different directions (see Figure 3). The Eucharist points back to Christ's sacrifice, incorporating you into his act of redemption and enabling you to give thanks for it. It also points forward, proclaiming Christ's death until his return and anticipating the heavenly banquet in the kingdom.

Partaking in the Eucharist is an act of community, both expressing and maintaining the unity of Christ's body. In this way, it points around you to other people. As a meal, the Eucharist locates salvation in the created order, affirming both the material world and our humanity. The arrow here points at you, as a representative of embodied humanity. Finally, the Eucharist points upwards at Christ, for in it you encounter your risen Lord.

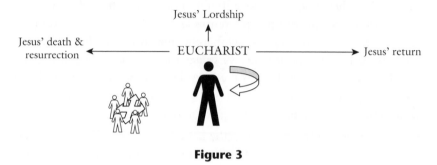

Figure 3

ACTIVITY

Read 1 Corinthians 11:24–34, Matthew 26:27–29 and Luke 22:14–16 for some biblical background to the discussion above. What are the implications of each 'arrow' for your own participation?

Baptism is mandated by Jesus (Matthew 28:18–20), and adapted from the repentance ritual used by John the Baptist. Baptism enacts repentance and the forgiveness of sins: in Romans 6, Paul indicates that in baptism you die and rise with Christ. Baptism signals death to your old way of life and birth into new life. It marks the start of your faith journey towards God's kingdom, in anticipation of Christ's future reign.

Baptism also signals initiation into the church community, for it unites us with Christ, and therefore with his body. This is tied to receiving the Holy Spirit, the bond that unites the church, so that baptism also signifies rebirth by the Spirit. Within the New Testament, baptism, repentance, belief and receiving the Holy Spirit are all bound together.

Section B

HEARING FROM GOD

UNIT III—THE BIBLICAL STORY

Your word is a lamp to my feet
and a light to my path.

Psalm 119:105

In our study of knowing God we have already been relying on biblical texts, and placing a high importance on what the Bible says. In unit IV we will examine such assumptions carefully. But first we will use this unit to attempt to get an overview of what is in the Bible.

We will leave until unit IV all the big questions about biblical authority and biblical interpretation, at least as much as is possible. One point is worth making now though: there are several different ways to approach the biblical books. We could consider them:

- in the order they are printed in our Bibles—which is a kind of 'theological' order

- in the order in which the events they describe happened—a historical order

- in the order in which the books were written—another kind of historical order

This whole unit will basically use the first of these approaches. This is the order of the books in the biblical 'canon'—the collection of 66 books that make up the Bible. It is sometimes called a canonical approach.

The aim here is to get a big picture perspective. Good sermons and studies can help us with details, but it is easy to miss the overall context for all the individual Bible passages we read and hear. So hold on tight: we are going to try and look at the whole 'biblical story' in four short studies.

STUDIES

9 In the Beginning

10 The Story of Israel

11 The Story of Jesus

12 The Early Church and Beyond

In the Beginning

The Bible begins with the creation of the world, the creation of humans in relationship with God, and the story of what went wrong. It then tells of how God called out a chosen man, then a family, and then a nation, Israel, and led them out of slavery in Egypt, giving them his law to tell them how to live.

Bible Passages: Read through Genesis 1–11, paying close attention to chapters 2 and 3

STUDY QUESTIONS

What do we learn about the significance of the divine-human relationship from reading the beginning of Genesis?

➢ What are some of the differences between the creation story in Genesis 1 and the more focused story in Genesis 2?

➢ How would you describe what goes wrong in chapter 3?

➢ What are some of the features of creation that are already in place before the problems develop in chapter 3? How might these still be significant for us today?

➢ What sort of themes do you notice from your overview reading of Genesis 1–11?

➢ What sort of themes are surprisingly absent from an 'in the beginning' story?

The beginning of Genesis tells us some of the best known stories in the Bible, though this does not mean that they are easy to understand. We need to ask why these stories were told in Israel, as well as ask what they say. In this study, you will consider several key sections of the biblical story: creation, the 'fall', the rest of Genesis 1–11, the calling of and promise to Abraham and his descendants, the exodus, and the giving of the law.

Creation

Creation in the Bible is about the importance of the relationship between the creator God and everything he has made: human and non-human. Genesis tells this story twice, in two different ways.

In Genesis 1, there is an emphasis on order and structure. In Genesis 2 the story is told with a very specific focus: the creation of the first human.

ACTIVITY

Draw out a chart of the seven (or six) days of creation in Genesis 1, noting what is made each day. What sort of links are there between days 1 to 3 and days 4 to 6? Now make a comparison with chapter 2—what differences are there between the order in which creation occurs?

People often compare the creation stories in Genesis with other creation stories in the ancient world (such as those found in tales like *Atrahasis* or *enuma elish*[3]). There are some key points of comparison.

- Genesis does not tell a story of conflict between the gods, mainly because it has only one God—this seems to be part of the point it wants to make.

- The creation account in Genesis 1 is carefully ordered, with reproduction 'according to their kinds', because in God's creation everything has a right place and a good use, unlike the chaos found in other creation stories.

- Humans are created in the image of God to work and to reproduce, not as 'slaves' who are to do the work the gods no longer wish to do.

It is obviously more likely that the author(s) of Genesis are dealing with the kinds of issues found in other creation stories of the time than that they are having an argument with modern scientific perspectives. So we note, for example, that the 'days' of Genesis 1 are clearly not modern 'days', since the sun, moon and stars do not get sorted out till day 4, but this simply shows that we are looking at a literary style of story-telling here. More interestingly, the 'sun' and 'moon' are not named in Genesis 1, but are called 'the greater light' and 'the lesser light' (v.16). This is because many

---

[3] Found in books like S. Dalley, *Myths from Mesopotamia* (revised ed., Oxford: Oxford Paperbacks, 1998)

nations worshipped the Sun and Moon, and not using their names is a way of showing that Genesis has no respect for them as 'gods'.

Once we accept that these stories are not simply 'telling it the way it was', but are stories with a point aimed at the people who would first read them, other things become clear too. In Genesis 1 humans are made last, as the 'climax' of all that is created. In Genesis 2, the man (singular) is made first, and the question becomes: what makes a suitable companion for the man? 'Man' in Hebrew is *adam:* many people read Genesis 2–3 as a story about what it means to be human, to be an *adam*. There are various important relationships for the 'man' in addition to the one relationship he has already, with God. A second one is with the woman (Genesis 2:23), which is described as a basis for understanding the importance of marriage. A third one is with the earth, or ground (which is *adamah* in Hebrew, Genesis 2:7).

The creation in Genesis is a place of peace, of life, of relationships, of work. There are no answers to questions of why God created, nor even of when God created, except that it is 'in the beginning'.

The 'Fall'

Something goes wrong in Genesis 3. The man and his wife hide from God (Genesis 3:8), which indicates a break in the relationships established so far in creation. The event described in Genesis 3:1–7 is known by theologians as 'the fall'.

ACTIVITY

Does the Genesis account use the word 'fall'? Where is sin first mentioned? Read through Genesis until you find the word.

The reason theologians use the term 'fall' is to highlight the fact that the human relationship with God is no longer what it was in creation. There is now a distance between God and humanity. This is symbolized in the story by the cherubim with the flaming sword (Genesis 3:24)—the way back to Eden is barred. Note also the cursing of the ground (Genesis 3:17): humankind will still be engaged in the work of creation, but it will now be difficult. And inequality is introduced between the man and the woman (Genesis 3:16).

What has gone wrong? There are a variety of ways of describing the fall in Genesis 3, because the passage itself is really very brief and does not seem to want to answer many of our questions. Fundamentally, there is an act of human disobedience, and a willingness to trust someone else (in this case, a serpent) rather than God. There is no discussion of why there was a serpent in the first place, or why a tree was created that had fruit that looked good to eat but was not to be eaten. (There is also no discussion of how the serpent could talk—the story has its own points to make and we do not get anywhere by asking questions it isn't designed to answer.) The passage simply wants to assert that something is wrong, the relationship is broken, and the world is no longer the way it should be.

The story is not mentioned again in the Old Testament (though there is a different version of it in Ezekiel 28:11–19). It is important for Paul in Romans 5:12–21 and in 1 Corinthians 15. In Romans 5 he makes a simple but powerful point: Adam's sin had consequences for all people; Christ's achievement on the cross will have even bigger positive consequences, for all people (and in fact for all of creation).

Genesis does not use the word 'sin' until chapter 4, when it describes Cain murdering his brother Abel.

ACTIVITY

Trace the impact of the 'fall' in the next three chapters of Genesis, noting in particular 4:7, 4:11, 4:23 and 6:5–8.

Genesis 1–11: The Beginning of Human History

Genesis 1–11 is one of the few places in the Old Testament that talks about the human race in general, rather than God's people, Israel. It is not a happy picture: consider the emphasis on sin, fallenness, human evil that leads to the flood, drunkenness, and the story of trying to build a tower that will reach to the heavens (Genesis 11:5). Despite all this, there are some positive themes too:

- the goodness of creation, as we discussed above
- the covenant God makes with Noah after the flood, where he promises never again to destroy the human race (Genesis 9:8–17)

- the fact that the people picked out in the lists of names and ages (Genesis 5, the 'genealogies') are just 'ordinary' (ancient) people, not kings, as in most other ancient stories of beginnings: the benefits of creation are for everybody and not just for the rulers.

ACTIVITY

Reflect on how you understand the balance between the good and the evil in human nature and society. How do we explain this? How does Genesis 1–11 help you think about this?

Abraham and the Patriarchs

The rest of the book of Genesis is taken up with the stories of the 'patriarchs', which means forefathers, or ancestors. The main patriarchs were Abraham, Isaac and Jacob, who was also given the name Israel (Genesis 32:28). Jewish tradition also emphasizes the roles of the 'matriarchs': Sarah, Rebecca, Rachel and Leah. The story of Joseph (Genesis 37–50) takes place in Egypt, and leads us on to the time of Moses.

ACTIVITY

Genesis tells its story through the lives of particular individuals. Draw out a 'family tree' from Abraham onwards showing how the major figures are related together in the book of Genesis. Note the way Genesis uses the phrase 'these are the generations of...' to divide up its story. This may also help you to get a sense of the plan of the book. (See Genesis 2:4, 5:1, 6:9, 10:1, 11:10, 11:27, 25:12, 25:19, 36:1, 36:9, 37:2)

Certain themes are important in these stories:

- blessing
- covenant
- testing
- struggling

The Abraham story begins with a blessing (Genesis 12:1–3). God wants to bless Abraham and this blessing will overflow to all the nations. God's commitment to Abraham is expressed in terms of 'covenant'. This is a legal term referring to a binding commitment. The main example of it in most cultures today is marriage, and the Old Testament sometimes compares God's relationship with Israel to a marriage, with its mixture of intense highs and lows, expectations and frustrations. The two main covenant passages in Genesis are chapters 15 and 17. You will see that the same basic idea is expressed in two different ways in these passages: God's commitment to Abraham and his descendants independent of anything Abraham may have done to deserve it.

God in the book of Genesis is portrayed as a God in a developing relationship with his people. Consider Genesis 22, which tells us in v.1 that God tested Abraham, by asking him to sacrifice his 'only' son, Isaac (i.e. the son through whom the promise of descendants had been given). Abraham passes the test, and God provides a lamb instead for the sacrifice. Abraham is understood here as a model of obedience, even in the face of an extreme demand. But it is also clear in Genesis that God anticipates, engages in, and in some ways even encourages his people to struggle with him. The story that shows this most clearly is Genesis 32:22–32, where Jacob wrestles a mysterious angelic figure at night. He received the name 'Israel' in this encounter. Perhaps this indicates that God's people 'Israel' are marked out by their willingness to struggle with God, and never to give up.

ACTIVITY

Read through the passages listed above for the four themes picked out here, noting ways in which they describe God's relationship with his people. Can you see something of your own highs and lows with God reflected in these stories?

Moses and the Exodus

The book of Exodus tells of at least two hugely significant events, both of which have featured as the closing scenes of major films, in suitably spectacular style.

The first main section of the book tells of the build-up to and the successful completion of the exodus event itself. The Hebrews are being subjected to slavery in Egypt, long after the death of Joseph. Moses is a Hebrew who ends up in Pharaoh's court after being placed as a baby in a basket on the river, to avoid the slaughter of Hebrew children instituted by Pharaoh (Exodus 1:16). He flees to the desert after murdering an Egyptian (Exodus 2:12,15), but is called by God to return and (eventually) lead the Israelite slaves out of Egypt, across the sea, and towards their own land.

You can read the songs they sung to celebrate these events in Exodus 15, and the whole story is retold every year even today in the Jewish festival of Passover, which says that every person should consider themselves as one of those in the generation who escaped from Egypt. This helps to remind God's people of their identity: they were slaves (to Pharaoh), but now they have been released, or rather, have become slaves to Yhwh (Leviticus 25:55). The New Testament picks up this same idea when it uses exodus imagery to talk about how people can pass from being slaves to death to being slaves to Christ. (e.g. Romans 6:20–23).

ACTIVITY

Note some of the parallels between the story of the young Moses and the story of the young Jesus in the gospels. Why might the gospel writers want to portray Jesus as a kind of 'second Moses'?

The second big event of the book is the giving of the ten commandments (Exodus 20). These stand out from all the other laws in the Bible.

- They are short, sometimes very short, and so are easily memorable.
- They seem designed to be generally applicable, not just in specific circumstances.
- They focus (in the first three commandments especially) on having God at the centre of everything.
- They set out the requirements for how society can function.

However, you should note also that the commandments are:

- specific to the worship of Yhwh, god of Israel
- not all easily turned into actual law (e.g. the tenth commandment, which is about coveting; it is hard to legislate about what goes on in people's hearts)

Should Christians keep the ten commandments? This is a specific example of the general question about Old Testament law for today, and there are various views. The Calvinist tradition sees the law as upholding an important ethical way of thinking and therefore (with modifications) applicable today.

The Lutheran tradition sees the law as a marker of how we never manage to live up to God's standards, and we require grace instead. Most other traditions fall somewhere between these two.

ACTIVITY

How does your own church or tradition resolve this question? Does it treat the ten commandments in the same way as other laws? Why or why not?

With the exodus and the giving of the law, God's people have been set apart as 'a priestly kingdom and a holy nation' (Exodus 19:6). The rest of the Old Testament will tell their story.

The Story of Israel

The story of Israel is a story of success and failure down through the centuries—of experiencing the grace of God as well as the judgement of God.

Bible Passages: 2 Samuel 7:1–17 and Nehemiah 9:6–37

STUDY QUESTIONS

What does God promise David through the prophet Nathan in 2 Samuel 7?

> ➢ Why is David not the one to build the temple ('house')? (vv.4–11)
> ➢ How long will the 'throne of David' last?
> ➢ Compare this passage with 2 Samuel 23:5, as David looks back at his life. What do you notice?

In all of Ezra's prayer in Nehemiah 9, what does he actually pray for?

> ➢ Why does Ezra think things went wrong after the exodus? (v.16ff)
> ➢ What was the (long-running) cause of the 'exile' ('you handed them over to the peoples of the lands')? (v.30)
> ➢ What is the tone of the closing section of the prayer?(vv.36–37)

The 39 books of the Old Testament are divided into:

- the 'Pentateuch' (Genesis to Deuteronomy)
- histories (two parallel versions, from Joshua to 2 Kings, and from Chronicles to Nehemiah)
- poetry and wisdom writings (Psalms and books like Proverbs)
- prophetic books (from Isaiah through to Malachi)

We will look at some of the different kinds of literature in Study 16. In this study we try to follow the outline of the history of God's people. We will focus on some main issues in the story, before finishing with a brief look at the question of history: did it all happen this way?

The End of the Beginning

The first five books of the Bible are known as the *Pentateuch* (literally, 'five books', from the Greek), although Jewish tradition calls them the *Torah*, from the Hebrew word for 'law' (or 'instruction'). After the exodus and the giving of the law, the Pentateuch tells of how the Israelites spent forty years in the wilderness, on their way to the 'promised land'. On the whole these were years marked by grumbling, frustration and an unwillingness to take hold of what God promised them.

This section of the Bible ends with Deuteronomy, which is a name meaning 'second law', referring to the fact that the book of Deuteronomy tells of Moses offering a second account of the law to the Israelites as they encamp across the Jordan from the promised land. It contains a second version of the ten commandments (Deuteronomy 5) as well as instructions on how to teach them and pass them down to their children (Deuteronomy 6). The book ends with Moses' death, but it does not end in the promised land. It thus leaves the reader still looking forward, anticipating how God's promises will come true in the future. This seems to be deliberate.

ACTIVITY

As we read the Pentateuch today we too must ask, how will God's promises come true in our future? How can we use the exodus/wilderness/expectation stories to think about our own spiritual lives?

Kingship

The books of Joshua and Judges tell the story of the arrival in and settlement of the land. Joshua reads like an official military history. It is an account full of descriptions of courage, battles, and lists of conquests. Judges is a much messier book, telling the scattered stories of individuals, and acknowledging quite a 'dark side' to the ways in which Israel behaved. A lot of the stories in these books make grim reading in today's world. But the book of Judges offers its own reason for this, in a refrain that also closes the book: 'In those days there was no king in Israel; all the people did what was right in their own eyes' (Judges 21:25; see also 17:6, 18:1, 19:1).

In 1 Samuel 8 we read of how the elders of Israel approached the prophet Samuel and asked for 'a king to govern us, like other nations' (v.5).

ACTIVITY

Read 1 Samuel 8, noting what both Samuel and Yhwh think of kingship. How does this compare with the view of the writer of Judges?

We see here that there is no one view in the Old Testament of whether having a king was a good or bad thing for Israel. History bore this out. King David was a ruler who, for all his faults, helped Israel worship and live in obedience to God, and he achieved things for the nation which could never have been achieved without a king. David's son Solomon was also a figure of internationally famous wisdom. However, during the reign of Solomon's son Rehoboam, in about 931–930BC, the kingdom was split into two. The majority of the twelve tribes formed the Northern Kingdom, known (confusingly) as Israel, while the two tribes of Judah and Benjamin in the South became known as the kingdom of Judah, centred still at Jerusalem, and continuing the Davidic line of kings.

ACTIVITY

Read 1 Kings 12 to see the cause of the division, which turns out to be not some major event, but a bitter personal disagreement. Also read Deuteronomy 17:14–20. How well did Israel succeed in avoiding the problems about kingship listed here?

The books of Kings tell the stories of both kingdoms and how they went their separate ways into exile. The verdict on kingship remains split: some in Israel still hope for the re-establishment of a king in David's line, while others think that the future lies with a different sort of leader. This is an important example in the Bible where we see that there is not just one view of something, but different views in conflict and debate. This underlines the importance of reading any one passage in a wider context to get the bigger picture.

The Exile

The Northern Kingdom fell to the Assyrians in 722BC. This story is told in 2 Kings 17. The Southern Kingdom (which now, confusingly, is sometimes called Israel again) survived several desperate situations during the reign of the Assyrians. In 701BC it survived a massive siege of Jerusalem led by the Assyrian king Sennacherib. This story is told in 2 Kings 18–19; it is also found in more or less the same form in Isaiah 36–37. This is because the prophet Isaiah was key in helping king Hezekiah withstand the Assyrian siege. According to the Old Testament, an angel of the Lord arrived in the night and wiped out the Assyrian army (2 Kings 19:35). The Assyrian records, which still exist for this period, tell the story differently: they say the Assyrians decided to go home feeling that they had been paid enough (see 2 Kings 18:14–16). Either way, miraculously, the kingdom survived. However, the way Isaiah tells the story, this incident is followed by Hezekiah showing some foreign visitors around his 'treasure house and storehouses', little realizing that they came from a new place people had not heard of: Babylon. Isaiah is unimpressed and predicts that the Babylonians will one day cause trouble (see Isaiah 39).

This prediction comes true in 587BC when the Babylonians, under king Nebuchadnezzar, attack and inflict another lengthy siege on Jerusalem. They carry off not just a large number of people, but also the temple vessels and gold and silver. Israel (the Southern Kingdom) goes into exile in Babylon. The books of Kings end on this depressing note. The exile also inspired much of the literature of 'lamentation' in the Old Testament.

ACTIVITY

Read the following passages that capture the shock and distress of the exile: Ezekiel 33:23–29, Lamentations 1:1–3, Psalm 137. How can we read a verse like the end of Psalm 137 in the context of the Babylonian assault on Jerusalem? Are such thoughts ever acceptable before God in such situations in our world?

The exile leaves a huge mark over the literature of the Old Testament. Most of the prophets are either predicting it, engaged in dealing with it, or responding to it. The histories told up to the end of the books of Kings are all building up to it, and are written with the knowledge that failure to honour God and live rightly would lead to disaster. The stories told in Daniel 1–6 are all examples of how faithful people had to adapt to the situation of living away from their homeland, unable to travel to Jerusalem to worship.

ACTIVITY

Read one of the stories of Daniel 1–6 and ask yourself: in what ways do Daniel (and friends) model living for God in a society that does not acknowledge him? What can we learn from him? What are our equivalents of King Nebuchadnezzar, the Babylonian gods, and the expectations of the king's court?

The Old Testament story does not end in exile, though some would say that it never really recovers from it. The Persians conquer the Babylonians in 539BC and take control of the extended area through which the Israelites have been exiled. They have a different kind of 'foreign policy' too: believing that if they keep people more or less happy then they are more likely to keep quiet and pay their taxes. The main result of this is the decision to let the Israelites go home and rebuild their temple. The story of the return from exile, led by Ezra and Nehemiah, occupies the later books of the Old Testament. You have already looked at the prayer of Ezra in Nehemiah 9. Many of these later writings convey a sense of trying to survive and keep hope alive.

The books of Ruth and Esther do not fit easily into our historical survey. They point to God's concern both for individuals (Ruth) and the way in which people are caught up in political struggles that have strong personal and emotional involvement (Esther).

ACTIVITY

The Old Testament world was very male dominated. What lessons might we draw from the way in which these two books focus in detail upon the role and significance of these two women?

The Temple and Worship

A lot of the story of Israel in the Old Testament revolves around its relationship with God, expressed in worship, and in particular in the importance of the priesthood and of the temple. There are actually two temples in the Old Testament. The first one, built in the reign of Solomon, is a glorious structure, serving as the one central 'sanctuary' where the high priest officiates before God. It is destroyed by the Babylonians at the time of the exile. The temple is then rebuilt under Ezra and Nehemiah, although those who see it recognize that it does not look as great as the previous one did (see Haggai 2:1–9). In fact this temple was not fully finished until Herod the Great, the Roman ruler of the territory 400 years later, invested in it in a vain attempt to get the people to approve of him. His rebuilding project lasted from about 19BC to AD63, but the resulting temple did not last. It was destroyed by the Romans in AD70.

The temple plays an important role in the books of Chronicles. As we have noted, these books re-tell the same history as the books of Samuel and Kings, but they give a slightly different perspective on it. In particular, they emphasize the power of praise and worship, and suggest that had Israel attended to worship more seriously, some of the things that went wrong would not have happened. It is significant that Chronicles ends with the permission to go home and rebuild the temple.

ACTIVITY

Read 2 Chronicles 20, especially vv.20–23. This is perhaps the most extreme example of Chronicles' view that worship could save Israel. What can we learn from recognizing that the Old Testament has two different versions of its main history side-by-side? What can we learn in particular from the belief that prayer can affect the destiny of the nation? (See, for example, 2 Chronicles 7:14.)

The End of the Story?

There is very little in the Bible about the events between the fall of the Persians (322BC, conquered by Alexander the Great) and the arrival of Jesus. The second half of the book of Daniel contains many encoded references to kings and priests of this time, especially in Daniel 11, which tells the story in quite some detail. The Jerusalem temple was attacked by Antiochus Epiphanes, the Seleucid ruler over Israel, in 167BC, leading to a Jewish uprising under the Maccabeans. This story is told in the book of 1 Maccabees, which is in the Roman Catholic Old Testament canon, but excluded from Jewish and Protestant Bibles because it was not written in Hebrew. It is nevertheless a helpful historical account of the period. The Romans conquered the area in 63BC. They too showed little respect for the temple, and so they too were not trusted by the people of Israel. The label 'Jewish' is used to describe the people of Israel from the Persian period onwards.

There were a variety of Jewish hopes for the future by this time. Some wanted a new king, like David, and in fact a lot like Judas Maccabeus, who would create a political revolt and throw off the Romans. Others (as in the books of Chronicles) focused on keeping temple worship pure. Some became experts in the laws of Moses hoping to bring about purity that way—they became known as Pharisees. Judaism today still hopes for the arrival of its Messiah. Christianity sees that hope fulfilled in Jesus of Nazareth.

P.S.—Did it Happen?

Our 'canonical' approach has focused on telling the story as the Bible tells it, though this has involved relating it to certain historical factors such as the relevant foreign empires. In one case we noted that there is an alternative account in the Assyrian records. But on the whole we have avoided the simple historical question 'did it all happen?' Some people see this as a major question, others as an irrelevant question. We shall make two (over-simplified) points:

Firstly, regarding what we do actually know historically, there is basically no independent way of assessing the historical accuracy of the early accounts. Only as recently as 1993 was archaeological evidence found referring to King David. This was a very brief inscription mentioning the house of David. We currently have nothing earlier than this. Many scholars would only start to date anything with confidence from the eighth century BC onwards.

Secondly, history writing ('historiography') in the ancient world is not the same as it is in the modern world. Modern notions of historical accuracy were not so important. This applies not just to the Old Testament but to all ancient texts. Almost nobody wrote 'just to say what happened'—there was always an agenda of one kind or another. But even so, this agenda would not have stretched to making things up with no historical basis at all. On its own terms, the Old Testament is as historically accurate as its first readers would have expected it to be.

The Story of Jesus

The four gospels all give us stories of Jesus, and all devote a large amount of their time to the events of his final week on earth. The combination of his life, teaching, death and resurrection make up 'the story of Jesus'.

Bible Passages: Luke 1:1–4 and Acts 10:34–43

STUDY QUESTIONS

Why has Luke written his gospel?

➤ What sort of 'sources' (other records and accounts) does Luke say he has used?

➤ Does Luke intend to 'replace' other accounts or add another one to the list?

➤ What sort of reader is Luke aiming his book at? What do they already know? How can this help us in reading the gospels?

Some people say that the Acts passage looks like a summary of Mark's gospel. (There is an early church tradition that Mark got his information from Peter.)

➤ What are the main points about Jesus which are summarized in Peter's speech in Acts 10?

➤ Can you think of any important aspects of the story of Jesus that are left out of this account?

➤ What is the balance in this passage between what Jesus says, what he does, and the importance of his death, resurrection, and post-resurrection appearances?

The gospels were not the first part of the New Testament to be written, which is why there are so few references to them (or the sayings or actions of Jesus that they record) in the rest of the New Testament. Nevertheless they are designed to be read first, because the story that they tell is central to what Christianity is. We will look at a few key aspects of the story of Jesus in the gospels.

The Kingdom of God

The kingdom of God is at the heart of Jesus' teaching. It refers to the rule or reign of God—in other words it is more of an activity that God is involved in than a thing or a place. 'Kingdom' is a slightly unfortunate translation of the Greek word *basileia*, which more normally means 'reign' or 'rule'. It is rare for the New Testament to use the word without specifying that it is the reign or rule *of God*.

ACTIVITY

Look up and compare these two verses: Matthew 13:11 and Mark 4:11. Also look up the following verses and ask yourself whether the kingdom of God is already present or future in Jesus' ministry: Mark 1:15, Matthew 12:28, Luke 17:21.

Matthew's gospel often talks of the 'kingdom of heaven', but you can see from the first two verses listed that he seems to use this as a parallel expression to 'kingdom of God'. This is probably because Matthew wanted to honour the traditional Jewish refusal to say the name of God. The kingdom of heaven is basically the same as the kingdom of God, and we should not think of it as a place that people are trying to get to.

Once we realize that the kingdom is something God does, we also begin to understand that it can be present in one place and not in another at the same time. The three verses you looked up give interesting insights into this. In Mark 1 Jesus seems to be saying that now that he has arrived, the kingdom is 'at hand'—almost here in fact. Matthew 12, however, suggests, that when God demonstrates his power by Jesus casting out demons, then the kingdom of God is already there, or in other words: God's reign is being demonstrated powerfully. The Luke 17 verse, which is unusual in the gospels, probably means that the kingdom is 'among you' (not 'within you' as if it were a human spiritual experience), which most likely means that the kingdom is 'within your grasp'. In the ministry of Jesus, in other words, God is powerfully at work.

Paul and the other New Testament writers do not say much about the kingdom of God. Some think that when Paul talks about the Lordship of Christ, he is saying the same thing in different language. This again helps us to see that the kingdom of God is about God at work.

It is important to see that, in the New Testament, the kingdom has 'come' (God is at work powerfully), but it is not fully come (we do not yet see God perfectly). The phrase often used to describe this tension in the New Testament is 'already and not yet': the rule of God is already established in Jesus, but not fully.

ACTIVITY

When we pray the Lord's Prayer, we pray 'Your kingdom come, on earth as in heaven'. In the light of our discussion of what the 'kingdom' is, what does this mean?

Jesus' Parables

Jesus frequently taught in memorable parables, using images and illustrations drawn from the everyday life of those around him. However, even when he did this, it did not mean that people necessarily understood him. Why is this?

Once Jesus spoke about a man who went out to sow seed and it landed in four different places. The disciples did not understand, and asked him about it.

ACTIVITY

Read Mark 4:1–20. How does Jesus interpret his own parable? Does Jesus suggest that the parables are easy to understand? Why does Mark 4:11 say that Jesus was 'alone' but then 'those with him' asked him questions?

In this parable about the seed and the soils, Jesus uses each kind of soil to describe a different kind of listener to his words. The seed is 'the word' here (v.14). This kind of interpretation is known as *allegory:* you match up details in the story you have told to something else that you are actually talking about. It is a kind of coded story. At different times in church history people have either thought all the parables were allegories, or none of them were. Most likely it is an approach that works for some kinds of parables—usually ones where there is a clearly important relationship between one person or thing and another. In the parable in Mark 12:1–12, the vineyard owner is clearly God, and his son is clearly Jesus himself (the vineyard, in a familiar Old Testament image, is Israel, or God's people—see Isaiah 5). In contrast, it is not likely that the parable of the Good Samaritan (Luke 10) is an allegory.

The second thing to note in Mark 4 is that Jesus says clearly that the parables are not clear! They only make sense to those 'on the inside'. Mark's gospel often talks about the issue of who is 'inside' and who is 'outside' with Jesus. The last thing that happened in Mark 3 was Jesus redefining who were his brothers and sisters. In Mark 4, the crowds who listen seem to be 'outsiders'. Jesus is 'alone' in v.10 in the sense that he is with his own followers—and this allows him to speak his mind about what he is teaching.

This brings us to the key point about his parables. Jesus tells them to force people into making a decision, for him or against him. The parables rely on being able to 'see' the point—they require a certain way of looking at the world. Do we 'get it'? If we do, then the kingdom of God might begin to make sense. If we don't, then it will probably just look strange. After all, who wants to follow someone who says 'The first will be last and the last will be first' or 'Sell all you have and come follow me'. The parables are memorable, which means that they stick with us, turning over in our minds, until their challenge jumps out at us and forces us to make a decision one way or the other.

> *Jesus' parables leave no neutral ground for casual interest or idle curiosity. They sharply divided their original audiences into disciples and opponents. They must continue to function in the same way today.*
>
> Craig L. Blomberg[4]

Jesus' Miracles

There is no single word for 'miracle' in the gospels, and this is because the way powerful and mighty acts were understood was different. In the modern

---

[4] *Interpreting the Parables* (Leicester: Apollos, 1990) p.327

world a miracle is a kind of suspension of the normal laws of science while something 'inexplicable' happens. In the gospels, however, they simply assume that God is at work all the time, including the 'normal laws' but also sometimes over and above them. Obviously, much of the time, things happen in predictable ways, but if God performs some 'wonder' or 'sign' or 'powerful act' *(dunamis)* then clearly the unexpected is possible. These are the words used to describe acts such as feeding the five thousand or raising the dead. In this sense, we could say that Jesus' miracles are examples of the kingdom of God at work.

ACTIVITY

Read the following verses concerning God's mighty acts: Mark 6:4–6, John 11:32–44 (note that some translations use the word 'miracle' and some do not). What do you learn about Jesus' miracles here?

One part of witnessing a mighty act of God is perhaps the ability to see that God has done it. Maybe this is why Jesus cannot perform miracles in Nazareth, in Mark 6? The gospels rarely address the question of why Jesus does or does not perform any given miraculous act. We might think that he would simply heal everyone, but perhaps it is important that the physical acts of miracles are not separated from what they signify. Note that Jesus raises Lazarus back to life after being 'greatly disturbed in spirit' (v.33) and beginning to weep (v.35). He is about to bring Lazarus back, but still he weeps. Is this because he is motivated by a deep compassion and an awareness of the effects of evil in our world? Miracles are not designed to impress in themselves, but to function as a witness to who God is.

Four Gospels, One Jesus

The word 'gospel' is a translation of the Greek *evangelion,* which means literally 'good news'. 'Gospel' in Mark 1:1 basically means 'an account of the good news'. The gospel is described by Paul as being the power of God (Romans 1:16)—it is something active. Perhaps we could call it 'good news with a purpose'. Although the New Testament itself does not use the word 'gospel' to describe its first four books, we use it to show that these books give us an account of the message of Jesus, God's message, as lived out by Jesus, with the purpose of encouraging faith (see, for example, John 20:31). Interestingly, the traditional titles of the gospels are 'according to

Matthew', 'according to Mark', etc. This makes the point that there is one gospel, but it is told according to four different witnesses.

ACTIVITY

The church traditionally associated four different images with the four gospel accounts, in a symbolism that lives on in church windows and paintings today. They took these symbols from Ezekiel's vision (see Ezekiel 1:10). Matthew was symbolized by a human face, Mark by a lion, Luke by an ox, and John by an eagle. Can you think of how each symbol sheds light on the different style and focus of each gospel?

The church has traditionally drawn its picture of Jesus from the four gospels taken together. It is worth noting, though, that each gospel provides a slightly different perspective on him.

- Mark's Jesus is a man of action, a man of the people, rushing from place to place, situation to situation.
- Luke's Jesus is particularly concerned about the poor, the outcast, the suffering—the people marginalized in the first century, including the women.
- Matthew's Jesus is a teacher who fulfils the law, and is concerned to set out at length new understandings of the old ways (as in the famous 'Sermon on the Mount' in Matthew 5–7).
- John's Jesus is the pre-existent Word, alive before Abraham (John 8:58), performer of signs and wonders with deeply symbolic significance.

The first three gospels are often called 'synoptic' gospels, meaning literally, 'seen together'. Their accounts overlap significantly. It is possible, as you saw in Luke 1:1–4, that Luke has researched Matthew and Mark first before writing his own gospel. John's gospel, in contrast, focuses on a few symbolic miracles, with long comments about their significance. Even the story of Jesus' last week on earth is very different, beginning with the 'farewell discourse' (John 14–16), which is not in any other gospel.

ACTIVITY

Compare Matthew 5:3 with Luke 6:20. Does this show us something about the different perspectives of these two gospels? Read the passage that follows in each case to see other similarities and differences.

Jesus' Death and Resurrection

Mark's gospel was once famously described as 'a passion narrative with a long introduction'. 'Passion', in this sense, refers to the suffering of Jesus' final week on earth, culminating in his crucifixion. Clearly the way each gospel is written shows that this final week has a huge importance in the overall story of Jesus.

You looked in Study 6 at different theories of how to interpret Jesus' death and resurrection (theories of the atonement). It is worth noting that when the gospel writers tell the story, in their four different ways, they are not particularly interested in offering interpretations. It seems rather that they were concerned with the basic story of what happened, and wanted to tell it so that everyone could know. No single gospel account tells us everything.

ACTIVITY

Skim through the four gospel accounts to see what each one contributes to the overall picture. Where do we learn of: the triumphal entry, the last supper, the night of prayer in Gethsemane, the trial(s), the actual crucifixion, the different 'words from the cross' spoken by Jesus, who was there, and who discovered the empty tomb?

*Note: it is not easy to fit every single detail together.

Throughout this study we have noticed that Jesus' whole ministry, in words, in actions, and in written form as 'gospels', requires a response. Luke's gospel ends with a story of how the disciples were helped to make that response.

ACTIVITY

Read Luke 24:13–35. How do the two disciples come to see who Jesus is?

Note that the two disciples on the road to Emmaus knew about Jesus, and knew about the empty tomb (v.23) and had even heard reports that Jesus was alive. But they still did not see how it all fitted together. Jesus shows them (v.27) that he was indeed the one spoken about in Scripture (which would have been our Old Testament). However, it is not until he breaks bread with them that they fully grasp the significance of what has happened. Our own study of the Bible is not just a matter of learning about the Bible. Our goal is also, through our study, to meet this God who is revealed in Jesus, and to know him more.

The Early Church and Beyond

Jesus promised that it would be to the disciples' advantage if he went away (John 16:7), because then the Father would send the Holy Spirit. The book of Acts picks up this story, beginning with Jesus' ascension, and tells of the early development of the church. It also provides us with a framework for understanding the context of many of the New Testament letters.

Bible Passage: Acts 2

STUDY QUESTIONS

What is the heart of Peter's long speech, and how does he tell his listeners to respond to what he has said?

- ➤ What is the symbolism of describing the Spirit as 'tongues of fire'? (v.3)
- ➤ Why does Peter quote the Old Testament so often in his speech?
- ➤ On what basis does Peter think the crowd should have realized who Jesus was? (see v.22)
- ➤ What does Peter say that he and the disciples are witnesses to? (v.32) Why?
- ➤ How does Peter say that the crowd can receive the gift of the Holy Spirit? (v.38) Does this apply to us too? (v.39)
- ➤ What do the new believers do? (v.42) These activities are sometimes described as key aspects of church life (along with vv.43–47). How far do you think they are intended as a description of what happened, and/or how far as a model to be followed?

The Beginning of the Church

Luke wrote a follow-up to his gospel: the book of Acts. Some have suggested that although the book is called 'The Acts of the Apostles' it could just as easily be called 'The Acts of the Holy Spirit'. It tells of the early days of the church, beginning in Jerusalem with Jesus' ascension. Right from the beginning of this account it is clear that Luke has a focus on how the gospel (the 'good news') will spread through the world.

ACTIVITY

Read Acts 1:8, and also Acts 2:39. What event actually caused the first disciples to move out from Jerusalem and travel more widely? (See Acts 8:1)

It is particularly important to Luke that the gospel will reach Rome, the centre of the world in the first century, in economic and political terms. Nothing could be more significant in the story of Christianity than that it should stop being considered a regional Jewish faith located in Palestine, and should establish itself in the main city of the world. Through the stories of Peter and the apostles, and then of Paul and his great 'missionary journeys', Luke shows this progress. This also helps us to see how Luke might have been writing for 'Theophilus' (Luke 1:3 and Acts 1:1)—to explain how this 'new' faith has come on the scene, and in what sense it is like the 'old' faith of the Israelite people.

> *Acts may be seen to be answering a complex question about Christianity. What is Christianity? If it is a Jewish sect, then why are all the Jews apparently against it and so many Gentiles in it? If Christianity is a religious rather than a political matter, why is Jesus called a 'king' and his movement a 'kingdom'—and why does it seem to cause riots and trouble?*
>
> Conrad Gempf[5]

---

[5] 'Acts', in the *New Bible Commentary* (4th ed, Leicester: IVP, 1994) p.1068

Jew or Gentile?

The key question that unlocks much of Acts, and indeed many of Paul's letters, concerns the identity of the people of God. They had always understood what it meant to belong to God: to obey his law (Torah), to read holy Scripture (the Jewish canon), to worship him, at special times at the temple as well as every day, and to be marked out as 'Jewish' in a variety of ways. Now other people ('Gentiles', which simply means 'non-Jews') were turning to God on the basis of what Jesus had said and done, and on the basis of the kind of preaching Peter had done at Pentecost. They had 'repented, been baptized, and had their sins forgiven' (Acts 2:38). They were doing all the things described in Acts 2:42–47. This raised an important question: did the Gentiles, in turning to God, have to become Jews? Simply put: how Jewish did you have to be to become part of God's people?

ACTIVITY

Imagine you were a faithful Jew at the time of Jesus. What types of responses to do you think Jesus would have provoked among your fellow Jewish believers? And how would they feel about Gentiles turning to God?

The book of Acts shows two very different Jewish responses to Jesus. The twelve disciples, like Jesus himself, of course, were all Jews. The crowds at Pentecost were Jewish (Acts 2:5). In fact the whole first section of the book, which takes place in Jerusalem (chapters 1–7) tells of a Jewish 'split' between those who did and did not respond with acceptance. Those who did accept Jesus could have harsh words for those who did not (such as we find in Acts 3:17 or 4:27–28).

The more complicated situation arises in chapter 8, where 'those who were scattered [by the persecution in v.1] went from place to place, proclaiming the word' (v.4). In this chapter we read of Philip converting Simon, a Samaritan magician, as well as an Ethiopian official of the queen's court. In chapter 10, Peter has a vision of God calling food clean that was previously understood to be unclean food. (Peter is mystified by this new revelation, which is an interesting example of the fact that the gospels were not yet available to be consulted—when Mark wrote his gospel he was able to anticipate this story in Mark 7:19.) This vision is to soften Peter up for a key meeting, with Cornelius.

ACTIVITY

Read Acts 10:27–35 and 10:44–48. What is Peter's conclusion about whether Gentiles can be welcomed into the people of God?

Peter's experience with Cornelius is a joyful one, so perhaps he would have been surprised to return to Jerusalem and meet with 'criticism' from the church there because of what he had done (Acts 11:2–3). One new convert who definitely thought that the gospel was for Gentiles was Paul (called Saul when we first meet him in Acts 8:1). Peter, Paul and the other leaders of the early church eventually meet at what is known as 'The Council of Jerusalem', in AD49, and recorded in Acts 15. This is the first of the great 'councils' of the early church, and the only one recorded in the New Testament. It sets out the answer to the question we have been considering.

ACTIVITY

Read Acts 15:1–21. What is the issue facing the council? (vv.1 and 5). What is Paul's view of this issue? (Note that Luke does not give us Paul's view directly.) What do you think Paul would have thought about Peter's final statement? (v.11) How troubling will Gentiles find James' speech? (note vv.19,28) What should Gentiles abstain from? (v.20) Why?

The decree of the Council of Jerusalem basically answers the question in favour of those who say that when Gentiles turn to God and turn to Christ, they do not need to follow the Jewish law (Torah). Scholars have long debated why the four particular things picked out in v.20 are the key issues for Gentiles. One theory is that they return to the covenant God made with Noah: these are requirements for the whole human race, and not the specific laws for Israel that we find in the covenant with Moses. Another theory is that they represent particular issues that were of concern for Gentiles at the time, perhaps to do with idolatry. Whatever the specific reason, the main point is clear: followers of Christ are not required to adopt the law of Moses.

In time, this decision led to a split between Jews who still followed the law of Moses and 'Christians', who are first called this in Acts 11:26 (and only two other times in the New Testament: Acts 26:28 and 1 Peter 4:16). Peter and Paul were both Jewish Christians, as indeed are many people today (often called 'Messianic Jews'). It is important to see that the New Testament is written during the time when this distinction is being formulated and is still developing. The issue dominates many of Paul's letters (see Galatians 2:15–21, 3:23–29, Romans 1:16, 3:1–8, 9:1–5; and the whole of Romans 9 – 11).

Paul the Missionary

After the Council of Jerusalem, the focus of Acts switches to the apostle Paul. His dramatic encounter with the risen Jesus on the road to Damascus is told three times in the book, to underline its significance (Acts 9, 22, 26). Paul's section of the book of Acts can be understood as a series of travels.

Acts 13—14	Paul and Barnabas travel around Asia Minor.
Acts 16—18:21	Paul and various travelling companions (sometimes including Luke, e.g. in 16:10) travel as far as 'Europe', called over in a vision to Macedonia (Greece) (see Acts 16:6–10).
Acts 18:22—21:15	Paul and others (again including Luke) revisit many of the places already visited, 'strengthening the disciples' (Acts 18:23).
Acts 21:16—26:32	Paul in Jerusalem, under arrest (see 21:33—this was predicted by the prophet Agabus in 21:10–14)
Acts 27:1—28:16	Paul is taken under arrest to Rome after appealing to the emperor regarding his trial (25:11).
Acts 28:17–31	Paul in Rome, awaiting trial

Acts ends abruptly: we do not learn the result of the trial. Probably Acts ends where it does because that is when Luke wrote it: he had brought the story up to date. In terms of dates, the time period covered is approximately the late 40's (for the first journey), AD49–57 for the second and third journeys, and travelling to Rome in AD59.

ACTIVITY

Look through Acts 13–28 with the aid of a map and the above outline, tracing out Paul's journeys and adventures.

Paul the Theologian and Letter-Writer

Paul's letters were mainly written as he travelled around the ancient world, including times when he was in prison (e.g. Philippians 1:12–14). They communicate specific points to specific people and churches. In other words, they are 'contextualized' to the specific situation Paul is addressing. When we read one of Paul's letters, we only have half of the ongoing discussion between him and the church: it is like listening in to one half of a phone conversation. We need to imagine some of what Paul is responding to and correcting in order to understand him properly. For example,

- the Galatians think that converts should obey the whole law—Paul responds that the law was only in place until Christ (3:23), and that they are now 'free' (5:1) and should live by the Spirit (5:16).

- the Corinthians think that because they have the Spirit, they are free to do whatever they want—Paul responds that while 'all things are lawful', not everything is beneficial (1 Corinthains 6:12), and he considers several cases where they are not in fact free to act in the way they have been acting (e.g. 5:1, 6:1).

In one case Paul urges freedom from restraints; in the other, restraints on 'freedom'. When we read these letters in context, we can see that Paul holds to some balance of law and freedom in his understanding of life in the Spirit. However, if we just took one of the letters, it is easy to imagine how we could end up with a one-sided message that does not do justice to Paul.

Does Paul ever set out his 'systematic theology'? Is there a way to understand the heart of Paul's message? Many interpreters down through church history have felt that the letter to the Romans is Paul's key theological statement. Why did Paul write it?

ACTIVITY

Read Romans 1:1–17 and 15:14–33. What is Paul's ambition?
(15:20) What has he achieved? (15:19) Why is he writing now to the
church in Rome?

Unlike most of Paul's letters, Romans is written in advance of Paul's visit rather than in response to issues raised after he visited. The time is about AD56–57, and Paul has set his sights on visiting Spain (15:24). He hopes he will be able stop in Rome along the way, though he is first going to visit Jerusalem with the results of a collection he has organized among the Gentiles to help the struggling (mainly Jewish) church in Jerusalem in the midst of famine (15:26). The Roman church is probably wondering:

- who is Paul?
- what does he preach?
- in other words: what does he think the gospel is?
- and in particular: does he think that his role as 'apostle to the Gentiles' means that the time for the Jewish people is past?

In short: Romans has a context too, but part of its context is: what does Paul believe? This is why Romans is sometimes referred to as Paul's statement of the gospel.

We shall note just two things from this magnificent letter. Firstly, the gospel is good news for everyone because it shows how the death and resurrection of Christ pay the price for sin, and fill the whole of creation with new life. The first part of this is summarized in Romans 3:21–26. The second part reaches a climax in chapter 8 where Paul describes the Spirit that raised Christ from the dead (v.11) now bringing about transformation of the whole creation (vv.18–25).

Secondly, the particular context that lies behind Romans requires Paul to address whether this good news is the same for Jews and Gentiles. His answer is a resounding yes: see verses like 1:17, 3:9 and 5:18 (where 'all' = 'both Jew and Gentile'). Chapters 9–11 express his hope that the Jewish people will in time come to embrace Christ in the same way as Gentile believers have done.

ACTIVITY

Look up the verses in Romans noted above and see how Paul
develops his argument concerning the two issues we have discussed.

The Rest of the New Testament

Other letters in the New Testament were written by Peter, James, John and
Jude. Books like Hebrews and 1 John seem to be more like ancient sermons
than letters. Letters as short as 2 and 3 John are actually more like standard
first-century letters than most of the New Testament documents.

The New Testament ends with the book of Revelation, which is an
'apocalypse': a word that means simply 'revelation', and here refers to the
way that John has a vision of God triumphing over the power of evil. The
end of the book anticipates a final victory over the devil and hell, and the
recreation of an Eden-like state of peace with God (Revelation 21–22).
There is even access to the tree of life again at the end (22:2), a final undoing
of the effects of the fall.

UNIT IV—INTERPRETING THE BIBLE

Take up the Sword of the Spirit,
which is the word of God.

Ephesians 6:17

The Word of God is living and
active,
sharper than any two-edged sword,
piercing until it divides soul from
spirit,
joints from marrow,
it is able to judge the thoughts
and intentions of the heart.

Hebrews 4:12

Unit III gave you an overview of the biblical story. In this unit we ask the question that goes along with any serious use of the Bible: how should we interpret it? Studies 14–16 look at some of the ways in which different types of biblical texts need interpreting. The name for this kind of study is 'hermeneutics': how we interpret the Bible and how we evaluate different interpretations. But to discuss the best ways to interpret the Bible, we first need to have a sense of what the Bible is for and why it came to exist in the first place. So we begin with a study about the nature of the Bible and why we have it.

STUDIES

13 Holy Scripture

14 Studying the Bible

15 Reading Poetry and Prophecy (Psalms & Isaiah)

16 Reading a Letter (Ephesians)

Holy Scripture

The Bible is both a collection of 66 books and also one book. In this study we ask some important questions about the nature of the Bible: how did it come to be one book, and what is its theological purpose?

Bible Passage: 2 Timothy 3:10–17

STUDY QUESTIONS

What does this passage teach us about 'the sacred writings' (v.15)?

➤ How does Paul's personal model contrast with those he describes as 'wicked' and 'impostors'? (vv.10–13)

➤ What does Paul want Timothy to do? (vv.14–15)

➤ According to v.15, what is the purpose of Scripture?

➤ What is being claimed for Scripture in v.16?

➤ What is the significance of the various uses of Scripture listed in v.16?

➤ What is the relationship between Scripture and the lifestyle Paul is talking about? Should we draw a similar link between our own use of Scripture and our own lifestyle? (note the result of using Scripture—v.17)

➤ This passage is written about the Old Testament (the 'sacred writings' of the time). How far can we apply it to the New Testament too?

The Canon

The biblical 'canon' is a collection of 66 books from Genesis to Revelation. The Greek for 'the books' (plural) is *ta biblia*, from which we get our word 'Bible'. When the New Testament talks about what we now call the Old

Testament, it often calls it 'the Scripture(s)', from the Greek word *graphē*, which means 'things written down'. How did this collection of 66 books develop?

The idea of a canon comes from another Greek word *(kanōn)* meaning 'rule' or 'standard'. The key point is that the canon measures whether a book matches up to the rule or standard: if it does then it can be included in the canon. If not then it is not included. This obviously begs the most important question: what is the standard?

For simplicity we will consider the New Testament first. The standard as the early church understood it was called 'the rule of faith', and it was an attempt to say what the Christian faith was all about. This rule, unlike the early creeds that we have looked at, was never formalized into one particular set of words, but it referred to the basic heart of Christianity.

ACTIVITY

Write down in one or two sentences what you think Christianity is all about. (This is an attempt to get you to spell out your 'rule of faith'.)

For the early church, Christian faith centred on believing that Jesus of Nazareth was Lord and Christ (Messiah), that he had taught truthfully, acted rightly, died and been raised from the dead, and that Christians should now, empowered by the Holy Spirit, seek to live out this good news in everything they do.

First century writings that empower the church to hold to this rule, then, are 'canonical'.

ACTIVITY

Imagine you are in a late first-century church and a copy of Paul's letter to the Corinthians turns up. How can your church decide if it should take it as a word from God or not?

In practice there were several 'tests' for any new document that a church might receive:

- did it have a link to an apostle who had witnessed Jesus alive?
- was it written for more than just its original recipient(s)?

- did it look theologically orthodox?
- was it proving useful in other places as it was taken seriously?

If the evidence for all these was positive, then churches could adopt the document into their canon. The view of the church was that such documents had been 'inspired' by God. At the time, of course, it was hard to tell just by looking at a copy of 1 Corinthians whether it was inspired or not. This view developed as the canon grew.

We can see that a book like Matthew's gospel was obviously 'canonical' and would be added to the collection, while a book like Jude might be harder to evaluate. Indeed, the evidence from the early centuries is that there was some disagreement around the 'edges' of the canon.

Taking a step back we can see how a similar process worked for the Old Testament. Here the issue was not to do with faithfulness to Christ and his teaching, but to the five books of Moses: the revelation of the Torah that formed the basis of Israel's life. Around these books came 'The Prophets', designed to help interpret the Torah for daily living. Around these, and with a title that shows that they represent 'everything else', came 'The Writings'. The Jewish canon looks like this:

The 24 books of the Hebrew Canon

Torah	The Prophets	
	Former Prophets:	*Latter Prophets:*
Genesis	Joshua	Isaiah
Exodus	Judges	Jeremiah
Leviticus	Samuel	Ezekiel
Numbers	Kings	The Book of the Twelve
Deuteronomy		

The Writings		
Psalms	*The 5 Scrolls:*	Daniel
Job	*(Megilloth)*	Ezra-Nehemiah
Proverbs	Ruth	Chronicles
	Song of Songs	
	Ecclesiastes	
	Lamentations	
	Esther	

These 24 add up to the same 39 books that make up the Protestant Old Testament. For many centuries, other books were included by some people: historical books like 1 and 2 Maccabees, wisdom books like Ben Sira, and stories like Tobit or Judith. As late as the sixteenth century, Martin Luther argued that since these did not originally exist in Hebrew they should be excluded, in response to which the Catholic Church argued that they should be included. In fact not a great deal depends on this decision.

In conclusion, the canon of 66 books represents a theological collection with the purpose of witnessing faithfully to who God is and what God has done.

One Bible, Two Testaments

The name 'testament' comes from the Latin word for 'covenant' *(testamentum)*. Our one Christian Bible, therefore, contains an old covenant and a new covenant. The book of Hebrews is an extended reflection on the link between these two covenants. Its opening sentence is a helpful way of understanding how the Old Testament and the New Testament fit together.

ACTIVITY

Read Hebrews 1:1–3. What is the comparison between the old way in which God spoke and the new way? What is the significance of Christ sitting down when he had 'finished' his work? (v.3)

Notice the parallel way in which the Old and New are contrasted here: once God spoke through the prophets, but now he speaks 'in' the Son. Once it was 'in many and various ways' but now it is in one way—in Jesus. The New Testament, therefore, is our way of understanding who Jesus was, what he said and did, and the significance of his death and resurrection. But the claim of the two-testament Christian Bible is that we cannot understand the new without grasping the significance of the old, and that the God of the old is the same God as the God of the new.

An important point to note is that the Old-New structure of the Bible is not suggesting that 'new is better' or that 'old is out of date'. It is a way of understanding how the whole of the Bible relates to Jesus. If new just meant 'more up to date' then we might imagine a third or fourth testament still to come, and some people do argue that we should be going against the New Testament where we have new understandings that leave it 'out of date'. This is not how the New Testament sees it: this 'new' testament is 'in these last days' (v.2) and the Son's work is now finished (v.3). The New Testament, then, is our witness to God's definitive word: Jesus.

Revelation

The verses from Hebrews 1 also help us understand the idea of revelation. To reveal is to make known what would not otherwise be known. How does God reveal himself?

ACTIVITY

Think about a person you know well. Ask yourself: what is the difference between knowing that person and knowing about that person? How are these two kinds of knowing linked together?

Hebrews 1 tells us that God reveals himself in many ways (in the past), but now uniquely in Jesus. The fundamental idea of revelation in Christianity is personal: God reveals himself. Of course God also reveals truth about himself. One of the ways we know someone is to know about them, and it is hard to maintain much of a relationship with someone when we know nothing about them.

How does God reveal himself to us? Hebrews 1 suggests that there are many answers to this, particularly in the Old Testament. People such as the medieval theologian Thomas Aquinas argued that the likeness of God can be understood through nature.

ACTIVITY

Read Psalm 19:1–6 for a description of God's revelation in creation, and John 1:1–18 for a description of God's revelation in Jesus.

Other theologians, such as the sixteenth-century reformer John Calvin, point out that only God as Creator can be understood from nature. Understanding God as redeemer needs some kind of special revelation, of what has happened in the incarnation, and the cross and resurrection.

John's gospel begins by telling us that Jesus himself was 'the Word made flesh'. In this sense, Jesus is the primary form of God's self-revelation. The purpose of the New Testament is to give us access to this particular divine revelation.

So we see that both Old and New Testaments function as revelation, because 'in many and various ways', as Hebrews 1:1 put it, they witness to the revelation of God himself in the Old and New covenants between God and the human race. Consequently, the church must concern itself with the reading and interpretation of the Bible, because in its pages God is revealed.

Inspiration and Authority

The terminology of Scripture being 'inspired' comes from the passage you looked at at the beginning of this study, 2 Timothy 3. The word here that describes Scripture as inspired is, in Greek, *theopneustos*, which we could translate as 'God-breathed'. As the American theologian Benjamin Warfield (1851–1921) pointed out, the issue in 2 Timothy is not so much that God has 'breathed into' Scripture, as if God decided to add his Spirit to a book, but rather that Scripture has been 'breathed out' by God. Warfield suggested we might almost say that Scripture has been 'ex-spired' by God, though admittedly this sounds strange.

Obviously we cannot explain the nature of Scripture just by quoting some verses from it—this would be a circular argument. Nevertheless, we should expect that on the rare occasions that Scripture does talk about itself, this should fit with how we understand the nature of the whole Bible. In the case of 2 Timothy 3, there is a strong emphasis on the practical contribution that Scripture makes to living a godly life, emphasizing characteristics like patience and love. If Scripture is a work of God, 'breathed out' by God, then we should hope that it will help us bear the fruit of the Spirit (Galatians 5:22–23) as we read it. How realistic is that hope?

ACTIVITY

Reflect on how you have experienced Scripture being used in church, or in Bible studies, or in discussions with others. Has it been used for the purposes described in 2 Timothy 3? What about your own use of Scripture?

One other New Testament verse offers us a sense of what 'inspiration' means: 2 Peter 1:21. This verse claims that when (Old Testament) prophets spoke, they did so because they were 'moved by the Holy Spirit' and 'spoke from God'. The idea is that the words of the prophet are their own (human) words and at the same time they are the words prompted by God. Prophecies in Scripture are fully human and fully divine, in a way that is similar to how Jesus is fully human and fully God.

Other kinds of biblical text work differently. The ten commandments, for instance, are described as inscribed on stone tablets by the finger of God (see Exodus 31:18, also 34:1—this is the nearest the Bible gets to the kind of inspiration that Muslims attribute to the Koran). The book of Proverbs, on the other hand, collects sayings that had circulated for a long time in Israel (see e.g. Proverbs 25:1, 31:1). Luke, as you saw in Study 11, researched his own gospel thoroughly from other sources. There is no one model of how biblical texts were inspired. The point is simply that this whole collection of different kinds of texts all, in some sense, come to us from God.

Because of this, the church has traditionally said that biblical texts have authority. Again, different kinds of texts will have authority in different ways. We can see how a law or command can be authoritative. What does it mean for a story to have authority?

ACTIVITY

Consider a biblical story—perhaps a story of God healing someone. In what sense does it have authority for us today? How is the language of authority helpful or unhelpful here?

Stories are some of the most powerful texts in our 21st-century world. When people read novels or watch films these stories can help them understand life, themselves and other people. Stories are some of the most interesting ways in which we reflect on our values. Biblical stories also help us do this—in particular, to reflect on our values in the light of who God is. The authority of the story, as N.T. Wright notes in his book on Scripture and the authority of God, is actually a shorthand way of talking about the authority of God in our lives. As long as we remember that 'authority' language is about God, through the Bible, rather than the Bible itself, then it is a helpful way of thinking about inspired Scripture and its role in our lives. To take an example: when we read a story of God healing, we cannot conclude that God will necessarily perform the same healing today. But we can say that we live with the same God today, and in this sense the story has 'authority' over our understanding of who God is.

Holy

All the different aspects of Scripture that we have looked at in this study serve to emphasize that Scripture is set apart from any other kind of helpful book or rules for living that we might use in our Christian lives. The concept of being set apart for (and by) God, in the Bible, is captured in the word 'holy'. When we talk of 'Holy Scripture', or the 'Holy Bible', we are being reminded that this 66-book collection makes up one particular book that is set apart for a special role in our lives with God. We should expect reading Scripture, therefore, to transform our lives, in turn setting us apart to belong to God.

ACTIVITY

Read Psalm 1. What happens to the person who meditates on God's word day and night? How can this be an image for us of what happens when we read and reflect regularly on Scripture?

Studying the Bible

We have looked at how Scripture comes to us from God, but what does this mean in practice when we open up our Bibles and start to read? This study examines some useful tools for the task of biblical interpretation. The next two studies will then use these tools in a range of examples.

Bible Passages: Psalm 19:7–10 and Psalm 119:97–105

STUDY QUESTIONS

What sort of study of God's word is envisaged in these passages?

➢ There are six things 'of the Lord' in Psalm 19—is 'fear' the odd one out? What does it mean? (see Proverbs 1:7 and 9:10)

➢ The other five things are all variations on 'law'—how does your response to 'God's law' (or more generally, God's word) match up to the attitude of the Psalmist?

➢ How does Psalm 19:14 link what we meditate on and what we end up saying?

➢ Who is wise according to Psalm 119?

➢ How does God's law taste 'sweet'? (v.103) Have you had any experiences that have helped you to appreciate its taste?

➢ What practical result does God's word have in v.105? How does this match up to your own experience, if at all?

The Biblical Text

The first thing you need is a good translation of the Bible. What counts as a good translation will depend on what you are trying to do: there is no single 'best' translation. Here we look at a few factors that will help you understand the issues in Bible translation.

The Old Testament was originally written in Hebrew (with a few passages, mainly in Daniel and Ezra, in Aramaic, which was a more widely spoken ancient language—Hebrew was basically a local dialect of Aramaic). Written Hebrew did not have any vowels. The Hebrew text we use today had the vowels added in many centuries later by the Masoretic scribes, and is known as the 'Masoretic Text'. This is usually abbreviated to 'MT' in the footnotes in printed Bibles. Most of the time the vowels were obvious—sometimes they had to guess, but these guesses rarely make any theological difference (an example is Amos 6:12).

The Old Testament was translated into Greek around the second century BC. A tradition that 70 translators all worked on it together led to this Greek translation being known as the *Septuagint* (abbreviated in Roman numerals as *LXX*). This is the version of the Scriptures that Paul and Timothy would have read and which is being referred to in 2 Timothy 3. The New Testament was written in a kind of ancient Greek (*koine* or common Greek), probably between about AD45 and AD100.

These texts were copied out many times by scribes, down through the centuries. There were very accurate methods for checking these copies— such as counting the number of words in the finished copy, marking which word was the middle word, and so on. The Hebrew and Greek copies we have today are not the originals, but are copies from much later. The vast number and range of copies (especially of the New Testament) allow us to cross-check and compare the texts. There are some discrepancies, but usually of a minor nature. Most Bible translations note them in their footnotes.

ACTIVITY

The two longest cases of different texts are the ending of Mark, after Mark 16:8, and a passage about a woman caught in adultery, often printed after John 7:52. Look them up in a translation to see what they say about these passages.

Translations

Translating Scripture began as early as the Septuagint (see above). The first English translation of the Bible (though from Latin) was organized by John Wycliffe in the late fourteenth century, and the first from the original languages was printed by William Tyndale (1494–1536) in about 1525.

A later edition of Tyndale's translation was thoroughly revised by a team working under the authority of King James I, and was produced in 1611 as the 'Authorized Version' or the 'King James Version' (KJV). This has had an enormous influence on the English language, and leads some people today to think that the Bible is somehow supposed to be written in an old English style. It has also influenced many subsequent translations.

Revisions of the KJV include the Revised Standard Version (RSV, 1957), and the New Revised Standard Version (NRSV, 1989), which has become a common translation for study purposes. The 'New International Version' (NIV, 1978) was a fresh attempt to translate the original Greek and Hebrew, and is good for public reading. Several translations aim for being easier to read, and worry less about being exact translations and more about communicating the point at issue (e.g. the Youth Bible, which uses the New Century Version, 1987).

ACTIVITY

Try to get hold of three or four different translations and compare how they translate some passages. What are the differences? Useful New Testament passages to look at are John 1:1–5, Philippians 2:5–11 and Hebrews 2:5–9 (which shows some of the difficulties of translating from one language to another).

In conclusion: when interpreting the Bible, try to have more than one translation available, check the footnotes of your Bible to see if there is helpful information there, and if in doubt, look up the details in a commentary (see the suggestions for further reading at the end of the book).

Genre

We saw in the previous study that the Bible is a collection of books of many different kinds or styles. The word scholars use to discuss these different types of literature is 'genre'. A rough definition of genre is 'the kind of text we are reading'. The word is sometimes used today to describe different types of novels or films (e.g horror, comedy...). Even this simple example helps us to see that a 'genre' can be culturally determined. For example, when we talk of Shakespeare's plays a comedy is a play where all ends well and the hero/heroine lives happily ever after, whereas today a comedy is a story that makes us laugh. The genre of a biblical text, therefore, is not necessarily going to be agreed by everyone, but it is a very helpful exercise to ask what sort of text you are reading. Basically, understanding the genre helps you as a reader to come to the text with the right expectations.

ACTIVITY

What sort of expectations do you have as a reader when you read a passage beginning with the following words:

Once upon a time...

In the fifteenth year of Emperor Tiberius, when Pontius Pilate was governor of Judea ... (Luke 3:1)

A man was going down from Jerusalem to Jericho... (Luke 10:30)

I saw the Lamb open one of the seven seals ... and there was a rider on a white horse ... (Revelation 6:1,2)

We can see that the reader will have different expectations for each of these passages. The first one is not a biblical example, though perhaps Job 1:1 is an ancient version of it? The second one leads us to expect a detailed (and accurate) historical narrative. The third sets up a story—no actual occurrence of a man going down the road is in view. The fourth one describes something fantastical—here we are in a vision of a very unusual kind.

The kinds of questions it makes sense to ask of each text will then depend on the genre. In Luke 3 we can ask 'what year AD was this?' but not in Luke 10. In Luke 10, which is the parable of the Good Samaritan, we might want to ask whether what is described is a likely or possible scenario, but in Revelation 6 it would not make much sense to ask 'so how did the horse fit inside the seal?'

Thinking carefully about genres is one example of learning to ask the right questions when we study the Bible. Some examples of biblical genres are story, parable, psalm, letter, gospel, apocalyptic, and prophetic oracle. You may realize that we were already addressing this issue in our survey of the Bible in unit III, where, without concentrating on it, we were careful to distinguish different genres. We will look at more examples in the next two studies.

ACTIVITY

Look up Amos 5:1–2. Verse 1 clearly defines the genre as a lament, which would lead Israel, as it hears these words, to expect an oracle about someone or some people who have died. Who is the oracle in fact about? How would this come across to Israel?

Biblical Interpretation

In this section we introduce two key technical terms: 'exegesis' and 'hermeneutics'.

An exegesis of a Bible passage is an analysis of what it says. It is a major part of interpreting, but does not go as far as talking about how the passage relates to us as readers. Some examples of the kinds of questions we might look at in exegesis are:

- who is mentioned in the passage?
- where and when does it take place?
- what is the genre of the passage?
- who does what?
- is it described in past tense, present tense or future tense?
- is it a description of something that happened or an example for other people to follow?
- is the story told with approval, or as an example of something going wrong?
- if it is a poem or song: is it triumphant, despairing, encouraging?
- is it personal or communal? (e.g. is the word 'you' singular or plural?)
- how do the different parts of the passage fit together?
- is it written for everybody or for a specified person/group?

You will see from this list that these are overlapping questions, and that there are many more we could ask. The benefit of exegesis is that it helps us to see what is there in the text, before we get too concerned about how it applies to us. But you will also see that some of these questions will not have simple right/wrong answers—they will depend on interpretation. We will consider several examples of exegesis in the next two studies.

Exegesis already leads us into interpretation. When we start to ask the question about how a biblical passage applies to us, we are looking at questions to do with how we should read this text today. The word hermeneutics is used to refer to how we interpret texts, and how we evaluate our interpretations. Clearly different cultures, traditions and contexts will cause people to evaluate texts differently. With the Bible, different church traditions provide an example of this.

ACTIVITY

Read Luke 1:46–55, Mary's song of praise (the 'Magnificat'). As well as answering these questions, see if you can distinguish between points of exegesis and points of hermeneutics:

—What is the occasion of Mary's song? (see vv.39–45)

—In the song: what has God already done for Mary, and for Israel?

—In the song: what is described in the future tense?

—How would different people respond to vv.52–53?

—Are vv.52–53 intended to refer to something God will continue to do in the future?

—Would you describe the song as realistic, idealistic, expressing a future hope, or what...?

Some people find it helpful to distinguish exegesis and hermeneutics like this: exegesis asks what did the text mean when it was written? while hermeneutics also asks what does it mean for us today?

Words and Imagery

In everyday life we know that words have a variety of meanings, and that just because one word like 'table' has many uses (e.g. a championship table in a sport; the table where you eat your dinner; to table a motion in a meeting...) this does not mean that they are linked together. It is easy to forget this in biblical study. The basic point about words is that what a word means depends on how it is used.

There is an example of this issue in 1 Corinthians 11:3 where Paul says that 'Christ is the head of every man; and the husband is the head of his wife'. What does the word 'head' *(kephalē)* mean here? There are various possibilities:

- to be 'head of' someone = to have authority over them
- to be 'head of' = to be 'the source of' (like the 'head' of a river, perhaps referring to how Eve was taken from Adam in Genesis 2:21–22)
- to be 'head of' = to be in a pre-eminent position socially, so that your status marks out both you and those with you (e.g. 'Paul's companions')

All three of these are widely debated meanings for the passage, and perhaps in 1 Corinthians we will never know which one Paul meant. Nevertheless, the right question to be asking is not 'what does the word "head" mean?' but 'how is the word "head" being used here?'

The conclusion here is basically negative: when we study the Bible we are not particularly looking for specific words, but are more interested in the concepts and ideas which the text is about: love, forgiveness, righteousness, and so on. Many biblical passages that show God's love do not actually use the word 'love'.

A lot of biblical language uses images, often drawn from everyday experience. Such imagery opens up a wide variety of possible interpretations.

ACTIVITY

Read Matthew 5:13. What does the image of 'saltiness' make you think of?

In his commentary on Matthew's gospel, Donald Hagner notes that all of the following ideas have been put forward for the image of saltiness: preserving, purifying, seasoning, fertilizing, as well as it being a metaphor for wisdom, or having sacrificial, covenantal or moral implications. He suggests that it could be any or all of these, and we should aim for a broad understanding: 'something vitally important in a religious sense'.[6]

Interpreting the Bible rightly does not mean that there is only one possible interpretation. Depending on the kind of text you are reading, there could be a range of fair interpretations. This is a separate point from saying that a passage has a range of applications, which is usually true for readers in different contexts.

---

[6] *Matthew* (Word Biblical Commentary; Waco: Word Books, 1993) vol. 1, p.99

Reading Poetry and Prophecy
(Psalms & Isaiah)

In this study we explore in more detail two genres that occur regularly in the Old Testament: poetic passages, which we will look at in the Psalms, and prophetic passages ('oracles'), which we shall study in Isaiah. Rather than start this study with a Bible passage to look at, we will take one example passage to study in each section, and then offer a further passage where you can try to apply the insights yourself.

ACTIVITY

Look up all the references as you go through the discussion of the book of Psalms here.

The Psalms

The book of Psalms (the 'Psalter') contains 150 separate compositions, collected over a long period in Israel's history. The title of the book in Hebrew is *tehillim*—'praises' (see e.g. Psalm 40:3 or the title of Psalm 145). In Greek 'songs of praise' was *psalmoi*.

Towards the end of the Psalms (from Psalm 104 onwards) the word *hallel* ('praise') is joined to a shortened form of the name of God *(yah)* to give us 'Hallelujah', a plural imperative that can be translated '[You! (plural)] Praise the Lord!'.

Individual Psalms often have titles that set them in a particular context. The common heading *ledawid,* in Hebrew, can be translated in a variety of ways, such as 'of' or 'belonging to' David or 'concerning/about' David. Psalm titles do not therefore tell us who wrote a Psalm, but they do indicate something about the Psalm's setting or purpose.

ACTIVITY: A STUDY OF PSALM 121

We will take Psalm 121 as a passage to study, and will try to model carefully how to ask the right questions of a Psalm.

> First: read the whole Psalm through.

Read it two or three times, and try to read it in more than one translation. If you read the NIV and NRSV you will notice several small differences, but nothing really significant. Note in v.3 that they have 'He will not let your foot slip/be moved' respectively. The point is that you will not stumble in your 'going and coming' (v.8—rearranged by the NIV to sound more familiar as 'coming and going').

We pick up the sense that the Psalm is about a journey. We also probably find v.2 familiar: 'the Lord, maker of heaven and earth'—a phrase that was adopted into the Apostles' Creed. The other thing you might notice on a read-through is that vv.1–2 are in the first person ('I/my') while vv.3–8 are in the second person ('you/your'). No one really knows why this is so. Perhaps it was designed for reciting corporately, with one person starting it off. Perhaps one person is drawing on their own experience to affirm others who are struggling.

> Second: describe the overall theme/story/point.

The most repeated idea in the Psalm is that the Lord is our keeper/helper (or watching over us, depending on your translation). This is affirmed in vv.2,4,5,7 and 8, and is raised in question form in v.1. From the beginning to the end, then, clearly the Psalm is saying that the Lord looks after us, and will not fall asleep on the job! (vv.3–4)

In fact, reading v.4 carefully, we note that the Psalm is a description of God's care over Israel. Can we apply it to ourselves too?

> Third: look for details that shed light on the main theme or ones that puzzle you.

The references to feet not slipping, as well as coming and going, suggest a journey. The shade from the sun and moon (vv.5–6) suggest travelling through the heat of Israel's deserts. Perhaps three details might make us ask further questions:

i)   why is the Psalm titled 'a song of ascents'?

ii)   why is there a reference to hills in v.1 and how does the question in v.1 get answered?

iii) what does it mean to be 'struck' (or 'harmed') by the sun and moon? (v.6)

> Fourth: once you have worked out your questions, turn to those who can help you: others in your study group, in church, or good books that will answer these questions.

You will need a good commentary on the Psalms to help you work through these kinds of issues. You will also realize, if you work out your questions first, how often a commentary (especially a short one) does not tell you what you want to know. In this case, you might discover that:

i)   the songs of ascents were probably sung as people made their way up (ascended) to Jerusalem for one of the annual festivals—probably going long distances in the heat and often preferring to travel by night.

ii)   the hills are seen by some as a sign of God's great creative power and a reassurance of his presence, pointing the Psalmist to the help provided by the Lord; although other people think the hills are where Israelites would have seen all the shrines to foreign gods against the skyline, making them turn to God instead for security in the midst of a difficult situation.

iii) the ancient world was convinced that the sun and moon could have deadly or evil effects on people, for example see Isaiah 49:10 or the use of a word for 'moonstruck' in Matthew 17:15 (often translated as 'epilepsy'), not unlike the English word 'lunatic'—'affected by the moon'.

The second question thus turns out to have no definite answer, although the overall point is clear. Is how you use Psalm 121:1 affected by our uncertainty about how to read it?

Fifth: reflect on how the Psalm's picture of God and God's actions speaks to us today

We may not be Israelite pilgrims in the heat, but do we also require God's protection in all our 'going and coming'? Does this Psalm encourage us to remember that God is 'maker of heaven and earth' (v.2) as a proper framework for seeing why we turn to God for help? Whichever way we interpret v.1, it helps us to think about how we draw strength from God in the midst of a dangerous situation.

ACTIVITY: NOW STUDY PSALM 23

Go through the same stages as above. Here are some questions which might help you focus stage 3, and which will give you plenty to look up at stage 4. You will realize that there is not a clear distinction between questions of exegesis and of hermeneutics.

- The LORD as shepherd—compare Psalm 80:1 with 95:7 and 100:3 (also Isaiah 40:11). What do you notice? Is the image designed to emphasize the complete sovereignty of God over his people, or is a gentler image in view?

- What do 'green pastures' and 'still waters' represent? (Are there several possibilities?) Were there still waters in the Middle East?

- The Hebrew word for 'my soul' (from *nephesh*—soul) can mean breath/life/mind/soul/spirit/person.... What is the point here?

- The paths of v.3 could be paths that are right (e.g. safe) or paths characterized by right(eous)ness. Could it be deliberately ambiguous?

- The valley of v.4 is the valley of *tsalemawet*, meaning either 'shadow-of-death' or (figuratively) a place characterized by such a shadow that it is as dark as could be imagined: 'darkest' valley. Is death in view at all here?

- For 'table', see Psalm 78:19.

- Who are the enemies? Do we know?

- 'Follow' (v.6) means 'pursue' (vigorously)—more likely to catch you than your enemies, perhaps?

- What is the 'house of Yhwh' (v.6)? Is it the temple?

- The last phrase is 'for length of days': is it more likely to mean 'for as long as I live' or 'for evermore' (as it is in some hymns based on this verse)?

For further reflection,

- what sort of hope does Psalm 23 offer, and to whom? Originally? Now?
- what images today might capture some of the ideas of 'shepherd'?
- Psalm 23 is often used at funeral services. How far does that capture the main theme/idea of the Psalm?

The Prophets

The main general point to make about the Old Testament prophets is that prophets spoke for God, and usually spoke to God's own people, about the standards God required of them. The word 'prophecy' is often used in general discussion to mean 'predicting things about the future'. Old Testament prophets did this too, but often the reason why there was a future dimension to what they said was that they were describing something (a state of peace, justice, ...) which did not exist yet, but which should exist, and as soon as possible.

On the occasions where they are foretelling something in the distant future, there is usually a clear distinction in the text. A good example is Joel 2:28— look this up to see how the 'Pentecost prophecy' is separated out from the other oracles.

Most of the prophetic books are collections of sayings, called 'oracles'. These oracles might have been given over a long period of time. The book of Ezekiel dates many of its oracles. They range over at least 20 years. Other books have longer time-spans.

Since the prophets were often concerned with practical matters of justice and lifestyle, we should recognize that their oracles must, in general, have made sense when they were given. If we can now also see a long-range fulfilment of them, for example in the New Testament, this may well be in addition to something that the oracle meant at the time.

ACTIVITY: A STUDY OF ISAIAH 7:1–17

Isaiah 7 contains several oracles, as well as one very famous verse (v.14), and also shows the importance of understanding prophetic speech in its historical context. We will select just two or three points to illustrate our study. As with the Psalms, you will need to consult commentaries to look up details.

Verses 1–2 give the historical context, though they are packed with information that is not easy to digest. A map is also helpful to follow the story. The nations and people involved are:

Nation (in v.1):	Judah	Aram	Israel
Which is:	the Southern Kingdom	Syria— to the North East	the Northern Kingdom
Capital city:	Jerusalem	Damascus	various
Also known as:	House of David		(Tribe of) Ephraim
King:	Ahaz	Rezin	Pekah

If you check the dates of the kings you will find that this is about 735BC. The reason that Aram and Israel have allied themselves together is given in v.6: they wish to install their own man as king in Jerusalem (these events are usually called the 'Syro-Ephraimite War').

The Lord commissions Isaiah in v.3, and gives him an oracle to take to King Ahaz in vv.7–9. Read the oracle.

- What is the basic point that Ahaz is to take from this?
- How did Ahaz feel before he heard this? (v.2)
- How do you think Ahaz might feel afterwards?
- Is it fair to use the last sentence of v.9 as a general word for us today?
- How does this oracle help you understand what prophecy is in the Old Testament?

Although the book of Isaiah does not explore this, Ahaz's actions after this oracle are described in 2 Kings 16:5–20. He actually contacts the King of Assyria, further to the North-East than Aram, and allies himself with him. This is surely not what Isaiah meant by 'standing firm in faith'.

In Isaiah 7:11–12 God seems to offer Ahaz a second chance for a word of support or comfort.

- In this context, does v.12 sound like Ahaz is being faithful, or stubborn?

Read Isaiah's next oracle (vv.13–17) and reflect:

- v.13 indicates the tone—what is it?

- v.17 indicates that the alliance with Assyria will backfire massively. What will happen? (note vv.18–20 also)

- v.16 explains that the two (Syro-Ephraimite) kings who have been worrying Ahaz will not last.

- vv.14–16 are the sign that all this will happen soon. How soon, according to v.16?

Verse 14 can be read as 'a young woman is with child' or 'a young woman/virgin will be with child'. The prophecy is that a young woman who either is or will shortly be pregnant will have a son called *Immanuel* (meaning 'God with us'), and that in the time it takes for this child to grow in the ways described in v.15–16, the Syro-Ephraimite threat will be over. This is in fact what happened: the Assyrians captured Damascus in 732BC, and the Northern Kingdom in 722BC. It is often said that the young woman of v.14 would have been known to Ahaz, and perhaps the child is his son, Hezekiah (here given a sign-name, Immanuel).

When the Hebrew text was translated into Greek, the word for 'young woman' was translated as *parthenos,* which does mean virgin. This is then quoted in Matthew 1:22–23.

- How does Matthew see the fulfilment of Isaiah 7:14?

This example shows that a prophecy can have both an immediate meaning in its own context, as well as a further fulfilment in the future. The book of Isaiah in the Old Testament points forward to the gospel of Matthew, while the historical prophet Isaiah was talking to king Ahaz in the middle of a war, where a prophecy concerning 700 years in the future may not have been the most important thing. The one oracle has two different settings and two different types of fulfilment. The idea that a prophecy can be fulfilled in more than one way is an important one in the Bible.

ACTIVITY: NOW STUDY ISAIAH 40:1–11 (AND vv.27–31)

Isaiah 40 is a good example of an uplifting prophecy that can encourage us as we read it today, but where it is also helpful to see the particular context in which it was first given.

Israel has been in exile in Babylon, but the exile is nearly over. The main route from Babylon to Israel was around the populated areas of the so-called 'fertile crescent'. In between the two, on a direct route, was barren desert—nobody travelled there.

The following are some questions to help you work through Isaiah 40.

- What is the tone of the passage? (vv.1,2,9,11)
- What is being said about the exile in v.2?
- What route back to Israel does God seem to be contemplating in v.3?
- How does John the Baptist draw on v.3? (e.g. Luke 3:2–6)
- Are vv.6–8 an encouragement for Israel? Why or why not?
- Does v.11 use the image of shepherd in the same way as Psalm 23?
- Why would Israel have been complaining in the way described in v.27?
- Who would have been weary, faint and powerless? (vv.29–30)
- The return from exile is prophesied as a magnificent moment (v.31)— would a verse like v.31 have been understood as a promise for 'every day' or 'for special occasions'?
- How much difference does the historical background make to how we hear Isaiah 40 speaking to us? Is this passage about Israel, Jesus, us ... any or all of these?

Reading a Letter (Ephesians)

Often when we read the Bible we do not get a feel for a whole biblical book at one time. This is especially relevant for thinking about a letter, where obviously the whole 'book' was designed to address one situation. In this study we consider the genre of 'letter' and then do an extended study of Ephesians as an example.

Bible passage: The Letter to the Ephesians

PRELIMINARY STUDY

Read through the whole book of Ephesians in one go. Try to avoid getting stuck on interesting or difficult questions: go for the big picture. As you read, look for:

> ➢ changes of style or mood
> ➢ linking words and phrases like 'therefore' or 'so then'
> ➢ repeated themes and words
> ➢ commands, requests, prayers...

One way to do this is to make a photocopy of the whole book and then go through it with coloured marker pens and highlight different themes and words in different colours. This will help you build up a more detailed picture as the study goes on.

This study will not answer all your questions on Ephesians, but it will try to show you how to keep asking good questions about Ephesians.

Genre: An Ancient Letter

As we noted in Study 14, understanding the genre of a biblical passage or book is key to interpreting it. Ephesians is a letter: in particular it is a kind of ancient letter. An influential classification of ancient letters (by Adolf Deissman, in the early twentieth century) distinguished between private and context-driven personal 'letters', and literary and public 'epistles' that would demonstrate considerable skill in argument. (The word 'epistle' comes from the Greek *epistolē*, which meant 'message'—originally an oral message, but it came to mean written ones too.)

Most scholars now agree that the average New Testament letter falls somewhere between these two types of ancient communication: being written to specific contexts for very practical purposes (e.g. to bring about a change in behaviour), but nevertheless written with considerable skill. The technical name for such skill was 'rhetoric'—the art of persuading and arguing, which was highly valued in Greco-Roman culture and studied in all the schools.

We will use the general word 'letter', which seems to be the best description of our written New Testament documents.

The Setting in Ephesus

There are two basic ways to investigate the context behind Ephesians. The first is to look up some historical information about the city of Ephesus.

ACTIVITY

Find a Bible dictionary or a commentary on Ephesians, and look up 'Ephesus' (there are suggestions for resources at the end of this study). What are the major points made?

You should discover something about Ephesus' significance in the ancient world, its location as a port city on the coast of Asia Minor, and also the fact that it was home to one of the seven wonders of the ancient world: the temple of the goddess Artemis. Artemis (known to the Romans as the goddess Diana) was a powerful fertility goddess, associated with new life, in whose honour magic and mystery rituals were performed. You can get some sense of how important the cult of Artemis was, and how Christianity was understood to threaten it (e.g. financially), by reading the story of the riot in Ephesus in Acts 19:21–40.

The second way to investigate the context of a letter is by what is called 'mirror-reading'. Mirror-reading is where we read a letter in order to see what sort of situation it reflects in the context it is sent to. For example, where 1 Corinthians talks a lot about matters of sexual morality and marriage, we can see that these must have been major concerns in Corinth. What emerge as major themes when we mirror-read Ephesians?

ACTIVITY

Review your read-through of Ephesians from the first activity in this study. What were the major themes?

Among the topics you picked out will probably have been themes like blessing (or spiritual blessing); prayer; grace; the Gentiles (and the one body of Christ); the church; power and spiritual warfare. This last theme makes sense in conjunction with our observation above that Ephesus was the home to the temple of a powerful goddess.

The repeated emphasis on the unity between Jew and Gentile in the church suggests that one issue in Ephesus concerned the extent to which Jew and Gentile believer were successfully living and worshipping together as one. This is a theme which we have seen in Unit III was central to much of the New Testament. If you now read through Ephesians looking specifically for what Paul says about Jew/Gentile unity, you will realize that it is a common emphasis, especially from 2:11 through all of chapter 3, and in the focus on living together in the more practical sections later on.

The Structure of Ephesians

ACTIVITY

When you did your read-through of Ephesians, what transition points did you note?

The major transition is the 'therefore' in 4:1. This divides the letter into two parts:

- chapters 1–3 —theological or doctrinal focus
- chapters 4–6 —practical or ethical focus

Within that basic distinction (which is common to many New Testament letters), you may well have noticed some or all of the following:

1:1–2   looks like a standard NT letter opening

1:3–14   is an opening blessing (it is, in fact, all one sentence in Greek)

1:15–23   is a prayer

2:1–10   describes something God has done (the key verb is in v.5)

2:11–21   appears to explain something further about what has been described

3:1   starts to describe Paul's prayer, but gets interrupted by:

3:2–13   reflects on Paul's own ministry

3:14–21   Paul finally gets to his prayer!

The second half is harder to describe in neat sections, though the opening six verses are clearly designed as a kind of introduction. One way of dividing it up might be:

4:1–6   exhortation to live in unity

4:7–16   'but'—this does not mean we are all the same

4:17 – 6:9 living the new life (not the old), in various situations/ relationships

6:10–20   putting on the armour of God

6:21–23   closing details and blessing

This gives us a basic grasp of how the letter fits together, although many details will still be unclear. However, we now have enough of a framework to move on to a 'second read-through'. This time we can already be on the look out for specific themes as we go through it. Colour-coding a photocopied text might be especially useful this time.

ACTIVITY

Read through Ephesians a second time, keeping a specific look-out for some of the themes we have begun to see in the letter. For example, you might mark passages that look at:

—issues of power/conflicts of power (warfare etc)

—wisdom or mystery

—the Jew/Gentile issue

—unity

—the church being God's new way of organizing humanity

(There are obviously many other themes to explore—feel free to add them to this list.)

Reading the Details in Context

Now that we are looking at Ephesians in its context, we can begin to see how some verses of the letter come alive. Here are a few examples you may have spotted as you went through, and which you should look up as we discuss them:

1:3   'Blessed be the God and Father of our Lord Jesus Christ, who has blessed us in Christ with every spiritual blessing in the heavenly places'

   —note that God is identified as the particular God and Father of Jesus. Paul does not want this God confused with Artemis (this is a frequent issue - see e.g. 1:17)

   —note that this God has given us 'every' spiritual blessing—none of the blessings of Artemis are worth considering

   —note that the blessings have been given 'in the heavenly places', and not in the temple of Artemis (see also 1:20 and 2:6)

1:8,17 'all wisdom and insight' and 'a spirit of wisdom and revelation'

   —note that in contrast to the supposed wisdom of Artemis, all wisdom comes from God (see also 3:10)

1:9 'he has made known to us the mystery of his will'

—note that whereas Artemis was goddess of a 'mystery' religion, which required special secret knowledge in order to participate, here believers in Christ have been invited to know the whole divine plan (see also 3:3–5 and 6:19)

3:16–19 is a prayer that we may be 'strengthened … with power' and grasp 'the breadth and length and height and depth' and love of Christ

—note that this is a vision of a 'huge' Christ, suitable for overcoming the other spiritual powers to be found in Ephesus

Genre and Setting: Further Reflections

You may skip this section if you want to get on with the study of Ephesians. Here we acknowledge two points which complicate the kind of study we are doing, and which you will come across as soon as you do any further study of Ephesians.

Firstly, as the NRSV and NIV note in their footnotes, where Ephesians 1:1 says 'To the saints who are in Ephesus and are faithful in Christ Jesus', some early versions of the copied manuscripts of Ephesians omit the words 'in Ephesus'. Some scholars therefore argue that what we have here is actually a general letter intended for Asia Minor, and it just so happens that we have copies of the version of it that was sent to Ephesus. One implication of this would be that the letter is not necessarily so obviously aimed at what is going on in Ephesus (though since Ephesus was such a prominent city this would still not make it impossible that the letter had it in mind). In our judgement, reading Ephesians against the background of Ephesus still makes sense, but it is only fair to note that this is a disputed question (we should also note that it is not in general disputed for other NT letters).

Secondly, there has been scholarly debate over the past two centuries about whether in fact Paul wrote it. We note here that Ephesians and Colossians are very similar, and some argue that this letter is written by one of Paul's followers, perhaps based on the language and ideas of Colossians. We do not have space to address this issue, which concerns the topic of 'pseudonymity' (writing a letter in someone else's name), and recommend the further reading if you want to follow it up. Arguably it does not make much difference most of the time whether Paul wrote it or someone wrote it in Paul's name—it certainly does not affect the kinds of points we are looking at in this study.

Studying a Theme in Ephesians in Context: The Importance of Unity

Ephesians 4:1–6 is a very practical call to live together in love, unity and peace. Paul even seems to suggest that this reflects the fact that there is one Lord and one God. Indeed, as he wrote elsewhere, if we are all divided among ourselves then that would suggest that Christ is divided (see 1 Corinthians 1:10–13, and note also that the church is described as Christ's body in Ephesians 1:22–23). Reading Ephesians in context helps us to see why unity becomes so central to Paul's thinking, and in particular, why it is a unity in the one church made up of Jew and Gentile that matters so much.

The following are study questions to help you reflect on unity in this letter.

- How is unity in the body related to our own individual spiritual maturity? (4:13)

- Who are the two groups being talked about in 2:14? (read 2:11–22)

- How are Gentiles described in their 'former lives' in 2:12 and 2:19?

- 2:20–22 describes the resulting church: what is its significance for God? (2:22)

- What does this newly unified church proclaim in the spiritual battle now going on in Ephesus, according to 3:10?

3:9 and 3:11 make clear that this unity was God's plan all along, but that it is newly revealed. This emphasis also explains why, in 3:21, we find Paul praying 'to him [the Father] be glory in the church'—the importance of the church as one unified body is that it makes a statement to the spiritual powers regarding the power of the healing gospel of Christ. The unity of the church is not just a matter of practical human relationships and how we live on earth; preserving the unity of the church is part of the spiritual battle.

Studying a Passage in Ephesians in Context: Ephesians 6:10–20—'The Armour of God'

This well-known passage takes on new relevance when we see it as part of the overall argument of Ephesians. It is full of imperatives—things we are commanded to do: be strong! put on! take up! stand! pray!

ACTIVITY

Go through the passage and note down the six elements of spiritual armour described here. Compare this with a passage that describes God fighting for Israel: Isaiah 59:15b–19. What do you notice?

We shall note just three things about this passage here.

- Firstly, Ephesians 6:12 cannot be emphasized too strongly: the battle is against the spiritual forces of our age and not against 'blood and flesh' (which is an unusual way of saying human beings, but that is clearly what it means). Given that the church has not always successfully limited its understanding of military imagery to the spiritual realm, it is important to note this. It fits entirely with the theme in Ephesians of the conflict between the God of Jesus Christ on the one side and the power of Artemis and other gods and goddesses on the other.

- Secondly, in the context of Ephesians, it is not individuals on their own who are each commanded to clothe themselves in the armour of God, but it is the church as a whole. Not only are the imperative verbs all plural—Be strong (all of you)! Put on the armour (all of you)!— but Ephesians has made it clear throughout that it is the church as a unified whole that takes its stand in the spiritual battle.

- Thirdly, this armour is in fact God's armour—he 'wore it' in Isaiah 59 in the context of fighting evil and injustice, and here he passes it to the church to wear. In other words, this is a symbolic way of describing how we (as a church) take our part on God's side in the conflict with 'the wiles of the devil' (6:11).

At the end of this passage, Paul appeals for prayer for the making known of the mystery of the gospel. This is a confident passage, with a practical focus, but it is realistic about the difficulties of Christian ministry. Note that it ends with a brief acknowledgement that Paul is imprisoned because of his work (6:20).

> ## *ACTIVITY*
>
> Go back and read through Ephesians one more time. Look for further details highlighting the importance of unity, and the emphasis on fighting God's battle against spiritual powers.

As you read, you will note further themes, which will in turn lead you to further studies. Welcome to the richly rewarding task of always seeking to travel more deeply into God's word, and always realizing how much more there is to know.

Further Resources for Studying Ephesians

If you have enjoyed beginning to look at Ephesians in this study, there are several useful reference works and commentaries that will help you go further:

Tom Wright, *Paul for Everyone: The Prison Letters* (London: SPCK, 2002) pp.1–80 on 'Ephesians'—a helpful devotional commentary written by a leading NT scholar

Larry Kreitzer, *The Epistle to the Ephesians* (Epworth Commentaries; Peterborough: Epworth, 1997)—a brief scholarly work, with practical emphasis

Peter T. O'Brien, *The Letter to the Ephesians* (Pillar NT Commentaries; Eerdmans/Apollos, 1999)—more detailed technical study

Gerald F. Hawthorne, Ralph P. Martin & Daniel G. Reid (eds.), *Dictionary of Paul and His Letters* (Leicester & Downers Grove, IL: IVP, 1993)—see for example the articles on Ephesus; Ephesians; Church; Power; and 'Principalities and Powers'.

Section C

LIVING IN GOD'S WORLD

UNIT V—MISSION: SHARING THE GOOD NEWS

You are the light of the world.
A city built on a hill cannot be hid.
No one after lighting a lamp puts it
under a bushel basket,
but on the lampstand, and it gives
light to all in the house.
In the same way,
let your light shine before others,
so that they may see your good works
and give glory to your
Father in heaven.

Matthew 5:14–16

The time has come to look at the world around you and ask about your role in it as one of God's people. The label that is usually given to this involvement is mission. The four studies in this unit will guide you to think about your understanding of mission.

STUDIES

17 God's Mission

18 Our Response: Evangelism, Community and Service

19 The Gospel in Context

20 The Uniqueness of Jesus

God's Mission

We begin by considering God's mission to the world. To understand our role in the world, we must first think through the meaning of mission and God's purposes in it.

Bible passage: John 3:1–21

STUDY QUESTIONS

What does this passage tell you about God's mission to humanity?

> - In vv.3–6, who provides the new birth that enables people to enter the kingdom?
> - How does Jesus describe the birth that comes from the Spirit, and what are the implications of this for the Christian life? (vv.7–8)
> - Who comes down from heaven and how does he enable people to receive this new birth? (vv.11–15)—note that 'lifted up' is a reference to Jesus' death
> - Who sends Jesus and why is he sent? (vv.16–17)
> - What is the result for humanity? (vv.18–21)

Introduction

Mission: God's work or ours? A job for full-time Christian workers or a part of Christian discipleship? Many Christians, when they hear the word 'mission', think of service abroad: mission is something that is done by Christians who move to other countries to serve God.

ACTIVITY

What do you think of when you hear the word 'mission'?

This idea, of defining mission as overseas Christian service, has been challenged by a massive shift in the practice of mission over the last few decades. Once it was possible, even if undesirable, to think in terms of a world map divided into 'us' and 'them': the great Christianized sending countries, and the needy un-reached lands full of people needing to hear the gospel. Such a view reached its height at the beginning of the twentieth century in a mood of optimism amongst Western nations that increased effort was all that was needed to finish the work of global mission.

Many factors changed to destroy the mood of optimism. Not least of these was the outbreak of World War I in 1914. Equally, as the twentieth century progressed it became obvious that Western countries, while often technologically and scientifically 'developed', were frequently morally and spiritually compromised. A century later, the church now seems to be growing in every continent except Europe, and to be nowhere more struggling and disillusioned than in the West. The 'third world' of old has become the 'two-thirds world' or 'the majority world' and is as much a sending area as a receiving area. Christianity is a global phenomenon, and God's mission is to the entire globe.

What is Mission?

Defining mission with reference to location is too limited. Consider for a moment the word 'mission'. It comes from the Latin root *misse* which means 'to send'. This immediately raises a few questions: who sends? who is sent? where are they sent to? and why are they sent?

The one who sends is God. Missiologists use the phrase *missio Dei* ('mission of God') to make this point. Mission is always, ultimately, God's work. The word 'mission' is a way of summarizing how God acts towards the world and humanity in particular. The church exists because of God's mission to reach out to humanity.

Mission derives from the very nature of God. Because God loves people, he acts for their salvation. As John 3:16 asserts, 'For God so loved the world that he gave his only Son, so that everyone who believes in him may not perish but may have eternal life'. Mission is an expression of God's love.

ACTIVITY

Do you take God to people? Or is God the one taking you? What are the implications of this for your witness as a Christian?

Who then does God send? John 3 continues, 'God did not send the Son into the world to condemn the world, but in order that the world might be saved through him' (v.17). The one sent is Jesus. Specifically, here, Jesus is sent for the redemption of humanity. Jesus is God's mission to the world.

This passage also addresses the two other questions raised above, though it does not provide a full answer to them. The purpose of mission, says John's gospel, is salvation, and this takes place in the 'world'. The word 'world' *(kosmos)* is a good example of a word that is used with a variety of different meanings in the Bible (recall our discussion of 'word studies' in Study 14). In John's gospel, 'world' tends to mean humanity, or the creation understood in human terms (contrast the positive and more general use of the word in Acts 17:24, for example). The 'salvation of the world' in John 3 refers to human beings being saved.

The focus of mission, then, is upon God bringing about salvation. As you saw in Study 6, the aim of this salvation is the redemption of humanity as well as the liberation of all of God's created order from the bondage to sin.

Jesus, the one sent into the world, becomes the sending one. Whom does Jesus send? His followers.

ACTIVITY

In John 20:21, what link does Jesus draw between the Father's sending and his sending?

The Father sends the Son and the Son sends his disciples. Like Jesus, his followers are sent into the world, and the purpose of their mission is salvation. However, unlike Jesus, his followers are not the source of salvation, instead, their purpose is to testify to it. The church's role in mission is to point to God and to represent him to a fallen world.

This means that the church is part of God's salvation plan. As the missiologist David Bosch puts it, the life and work of the church 'are intimately bound up with God's cosmic-historical plan for the salvation of the world'.[7] The church is the sent one. It is God who sends the church into the world, to play a role in fulfilling his purposes. Mission is what the church does in the world when it is being the church, or as Bosch expresses it: 'Mission is the Church sent into the world, to love, to serve, to preach, to teach, to heal, to liberate.'[8]

If mission is the church at work in the world, then it is not just for special people who are set apart in some way to serve God. Mission is for all of us. It has to do with how we live out our lives as Christians. As God's tool for mission, the church is not a fortress for protection from the world but an army camp resourcing our engagement in the conflict (recall here our study of Ephesians 6 in Study 16).

Nonetheless, God does at times set apart certain people for specific tasks.

ACTIVITY

Read Acts 13:1–4a. Who calls Paul and Barnabas and how does the church respond?

The Holy Spirit sends Paul and Barnabas out as apostles to the Gentiles. Their specific task originates in the church, is commissioned by the church, and is part of the overall mission of the church. It is not that Paul and Barnabas do mission for the church, but rather that they extend the mission of the church.

Notice also that it is the Holy Spirit who empowers God's people for mission. We do not testify alone. Rather, our testimony to Jesus' salvation is the work of the Holy Spirit in us, and in the whole church.

Thinking Biblically about Mission

At the end of Matthew's gospel we find a passage where Jesus commissions his disciples for the work ahead of them. This passage is often referred to as the 'Great Commission'.

---

[7] *Transforming Mission*, p.378

[8] *Ibid.*, p.412

ACTIVITY

Read Matthew 28:16–20. What does Jesus tell his disciples to do? What does this tell you about mission?

This passage is a good starting place for our discussion of the biblical understanding of mission, but we should understand that the whole Bible is a missionary book. We have a much greater mission mandate than the closing verses of Matthew's gospel. When we talk about a 'biblical basis for mission' we are looking to do more than select a few Bible verses that make some points we might like to make about mission. We are trying to grasp what the whole biblical witness, from Genesis to Revelation, has to say about God's mission to the human race.

> *Many Christians in the West 'have been preoccupied with the end of the Gospel of Matthew, the Great Commission: "Go and make." I call them "to go and make" missionaries. These are the go-and-fix it people. I would like to suggest a new favourite passage, the Great Invitation: "Come, follow me. I will make you fishers of men" (Mark 1:17). Not "go and make," but "I will make you."'*
>
> David Zac Niringiye, a Ugandan church leader

This means we read the whole of Matthew's gospel for its insight into the nature of Christian mission, and not just its last three verses. It means wrestling with how Paul viewed the nature of mission to the whole creation in Romans, and not just memorizing one or two verses about sin and eternal life. It means understanding the implications of Israel's calling throughout the Old Testament as well as the few explicit words God spoke to Abraham in Genesis 12. As Christopher Wright puts it: 'the whole Bible renders to us the story of God's mission through God's people in their engagement with God's world for the sake of the whole of God's creation.'[9] You saw a little in unit III of how the overall biblical story works in this way. Here we review some aspects of this story with a specific focus on mission.

God's mission begins early in Genesis. God made humanity to be in relationship with him and with each other. The fall damages these relationships, bringing separation, from God and from one another. God's response to this situation is mission: he seeks to restore humanity to himself,

---

[9] *The Mission of God*, p.51

and he does this *through* humanity. God calls Abraham, initiating his mission to the world through a people descended from one obedient, worshipful follower.

ACTIVITY

What do you learn from Genesis 12:1–9 about God's concern for humanity? Who sends Abraham? In vv.2–3, why is Abraham sent and what is the result for the human race? How does Abraham respond? (vv.4,7–8)

The nation of Israel, descended from Abraham, is called to be 'a priestly kingdom and a holy nation' (Exodus 19:6), testifying to the greatness of their God before the peoples of the world. As you saw in unit III, Israel struggled to live out its calling consistently, and was often led astray in injustice, idolatry and many other forms of disobedience. But God's purposes in calling Abraham did not end with Israel. God's bond with this people reaches its climax when he becomes one of them.

The turning point in God's mission to humanity is the gospel, which may be summed up in the person of Jesus. At the centre of the salvation story is God as a person.

ACTIVITY

Recall our discussion of the word 'gospel' in unit III. What are some of the things it calls to mind for you?

Christianity stands out among the world's religions because although its teachings are important, it concentrates on the teacher more than his teachings. The person of Jesus Christ is at the centre of Christianity in a way that no other major religious figure is at the centre of any other religion. Paul was a missionary not afraid to argue long and hard with all comers, but even he wanted to say, in 1 Corinthians 2:2, 'I resolved to know nothing while I was with you except Jesus Christ and him crucified.'

The gospel (literally, the 'good news') concerns God's redemption of humanity (and the created order) through the life, death and resurrection of Jesus. Jesus is good news for humanity.

In the gospel, God's ultimate future for the world is brought into the present. Jesus proclaims in his ministry that the kingdom of God has arrived and is present with him. Jesus' presence brings God into the world in new and life-transforming ways. His historical act of redemption provides a salvation that fundamentally alters who we are, right now, in relation to God.

But salvation is also an ongoing process that reaches fulfilment in the future. After Jesus' ascension, the Holy Spirit is unleashed on earth and dwells in believers, bringing new life and 'new creation' (as Paul expresses it, in 2 Corinthians 5:17). In the church, the seeds of God's kingdom have been planted and are growing, and the church is called to be a community where God dwells, a community that is founded in justice, motivated by love and characterized by peace.

Notably, Scripture does not conclude with the four gospels. The story of salvation continues on into the early history of the church, including multiple letters helping the church understand how to live out their salvation. After Pentecost, it is the Holy Spirit who guides and motivates God's people in mission. This happens in a wide variety of ways. You have already seen, in Acts 13, how the Spirit calls certain people to certain tasks.

ACTIVITY

Look through the book of Acts for different ways that the Spirit initiates and guides mission. For example:

—Acts 4:5–10—who enables Peter to speak before the Jewish council?

—Acts 4:23–31 records the prayers of the disciples after Peter and John's release from this council—for what do the disciples pray and how is their prayer answered?

—Acts 8:26–40—how does the Spirit guide Philip, and how much of this guidance is explicit?

—Acts 10:44–48—what proves to Peter and other Jewish believers that Gentiles can be God's people too?

—Acts 16:6–10—how does the Spirit guide Paul's journey?

Mission, like all of the works of God, is trinitarian. The Father sends the Son, the Son enacts salvation, and the Spirit enables humanity to hear and embrace that salvation. Peter takes the presence of the Spirit within the

Gentiles, in Acts 10:44–48, as evidence of their salvation. Peter's role here is to testify to the gospel, but it is the Spirit who is in charge.

What we are beginning to see, in this brief review, is that the entire Bible is a missionary document, and the more we understand it the more we are compelled to live out the gospel wherever we are. All that we do as the people of God is a response to God and his mission to the world. The rest of this unit examines areas that arise out of this understanding of mission as the living out of God's kingdom on earth.

ACTIVITY

How does it affect your view of mission to think of the church as the sent one, rather than the one doing the sending?

Our Response: Evangelism, Community and Service

Having established that mission is God's work, it is now time to ask questions about the part we play in God's mission to the world.

Bible passage: Luke 4:16–21

STUDY QUESTIONS

This passage has been called Jesus' 'manifesto for ministry', coming as it does at the beginning of his ministry as described in Luke. Jesus states here his purposes in mission. How does Jesus' ministry provide a model for the church?

> ➤ Who has anointed Jesus for ministry? (v.18) (see also 3:21–22)
> ➤ The 'poor' in this passage refers to anyone with low status, whether as a function of money, education or heritage. How does Jesus bring good news to the poor?
> ➤ How might the 'recovery of sight' refer to both physical healing and the experience of salvation?
> ➤ How might liberation of the 'oppressed' signify both the forgiveness of sins and release from demonic oppression?
> ➤ How does the incarnation help us to understand v.21?
> ➤ What are some of the ways in which Jesus' ministry fulfils this passage?

The Holistic Gospel

Jesus sends his followers into the world just as the Father had sent him into the world. Jesus' ministry, then, provides a model for ours. There is an obvious difference—Jesus provides salvation, while we testify to it—but, nonetheless, the outworking of this salvation in the lives of people remains the same.

An examination of Jesus' ministry reveals what is known as 'a holistic approach'. In other words, Jesus would treat a person as a 'whole', and would minister to all of their needs, caring for their spiritual, social and physical well-being rather than separating off one aspect of them for attention. He restored sight to the blind and proclaimed himself the light of the world. He fed the hungry and gave his body as a sacrifice. He exorcized demons and forgave sins. Jesus was interested in people's well-being in the present, as well as in some future life.

Jesus' gospel is thus a holistic gospel. It is good news for the whole person, and addresses us both in the present as well as eternally, penetrating every facet of human life. As you have seen in previous studies, salvation has to do with our past, our present and our future. Consequently, the mission of the church involves caring about all aspects of the lives being lived all around us: about injustice, poverty, oppression, spiritual darkness, pain and suffering. The challenge of mission in our world is to respond to life as it is experienced. Mission approaches individuals as whole people.

For many years, missiologists discussed mission under three categories. The three classic elements of mission were evangelism, community and service. The first of these, evangelism or *kerygma* (proclamation), involves proclaiming the message of salvation in Christ. The second, community or *koinōnia* (fellowship), refers to the church being the message of salvation as it lives in communion with God. The third, service or *diakonia,* involves demonstrating the message of salvation by serving the needs of people. Holistic mission demands all three of these.

> *mission mandate:*
>
> *the whole church bringing the whole gospel to the whole world*
>
> missionary conference slogan[10]

More recently missiologists have expanded their definition of mission to include other categories. David Bosch, for example, argues that mission is multi-dimensional, as you saw in Study 17. Mission is about the church at

---

[10] Quoted in Bosch, *Transforming Mission*, p.10

work in the world in many and various ways. As Martin Luther once put it, mission is 'the church of God in motion'.

However, for the sake of clarity, the remainder of this study will consider the church's role in mission using the three categories of evangelism, community and service. We also further explore the last two in other studies. Although you should not limit your understanding of mission to these categories, they provide a helpful framework for thinking about the church as a missional community.

ACTIVITY

How does the early church demonstrate evangelism, service and community? What other aspects of mission does it model? Take a few minutes to look through the first 9 chapters of Acts, asking, what does the church do after Pentecost? You may particularly want to consider 2:14–36, 2:41–42, 2:44–45, 3:1–10, 4:23–31, 4:32–35, 6:1–6, 9:32–35, 9:36–41.

Evangelism

It should be clear by now that mission and evangelism are not the same things. Mission includes evangelism but is not limited to it.

ACTIVITY

What do you think of when you hear the word 'evangelism'?

'Evangelism' comes from the Greek word *evangelion,* meaning literally the good news, or the gospel. Christian evangelism is the proclamation of this good news: God's salvation in Christ. It is therefore usually, but not exclusively, something spoken or preached. Its focus is upon those who have not met Jesus.

> *Evangelism is one beggar telling another beggar where to find bread.*
>
> C.H. Spurgeon

The aim of evangelism is to bring non-believers into fellowship with Christ, and thus with the whole body of Christ. However, evangelism is not about increasing church attendance. Rather, it is about witnessing to the salvation provided in Christ so that others may receive it too. You engage in evangelism because of what God has already done for the salvation of the world, and because of how he will ultimately bring that salvation to fruition.

Evangelism is not about winning converts but about helping people to become disciples. Scripture does portray belief in Christ as a radical change in personal status via the invasion of the Holy Spirit. Once you were in darkness but now you are in light. The old self is gone and the new is come. However, Scripture also portrays the Christian life as a process of growth, as the Holy Spirit forms Christ in you. Discipleship is a journey whose destination is becoming Christ-like. It is a life-long process.

It makes no sense, in biblical terms, to imagine that once you have 'made a commitment' to Jesus it does not matter if you never follow it up in your daily life. To embrace Jesus' salvation is to submit to Jesus as Lord.

ACTIVITY

Read Romans 6:15–23. Notice how Paul classifies people as either enslaved to sin or enslaved to righteousness. Does Paul consider it an option to accept the gospel but not to submit to it?

The good news of Jesus brings about changed lives. Of course, only God can change lives; it is not up to the evangelist to 'get results'. Evangelism, therefore, is not about trying to convince people to believe a certain set of things. Rather, it is to help people meet the God who is Father, Son and Spirit. We might think of evangelism, then, as simply introducing people to Jesus.

ACTIVITY

What does it mean to ' introduce someone to Jesus'? How would you introduce someone to a friend of yours, in general?

One thing we can do is to let people hear Jesus speak, for instance by reading or studying a gospel together. Our role here is not to have all of the answers, but rather to be facilitating a relationship. Most people come to Christian faith gradually and through relationships. You can most easily introduce someone to Jesus if you already have a relationship with both of them—Jesus and the person who hasn't met him.

Recall John 3:16: the fundamental basis of God reaching out to the world was love. In John's gospel this did not mean that Jesus didn't have some very hard things to say at times. The balance of truth and love is not an easy one. Peter offers wise words about the need to understand the 'good news' properly but also to share it appropriately: 'Always be ready to make your defence to anyone who demands from you an accounting for the hope that is in you, yet do it with gentleness and reverence' (1 Peter 3:15–16a). Understanding the gospel rightly is important. We have spent considerable time on this in earlier studies. But remember, if we had to believe all of the right things before we could become a Christian, none of us would ever get started.

ACTIVITY

Compare John 3:1–21 and 4:1–30 for Jesus' encounters with Nicodemus and the woman at the well. In what ways does Jesus treat these two people differently? Why?

One important way in which disciples can witness to Jesus is to 'testify' or give a 'testimony' to the work of God in their lives. We should be able and willing to tell our own stories of God at work in our lives. Not everyone can point to a particular conversion experience or miraculous incident, but God has acted in each life in a unique way and he has given us our own experiences to share. Ask yourself: how has God changed you, and why is it that you believe in him?

ACTIVITY

If you are working through this study in a group, spend some time telling one another, perhaps in pairs, your own story of meeting Christ and how God has worked in your life. If you are working on your own, write out your story.

God will treat each person as an individual. If you have just done the above activity in a group it will probably be particularly clear: different aspects of the Christian gospel strike different people in various ways, and the 'key' that makes it all fall into place for one person is unlikely to be the same for another person.

Evangelism is the simple act of telling people the good news, and the evidence of the book of Acts (and church history) is that some will respond positively and some will respond negatively. Do not force people into a response. On the other hand, someone may want to become a Christian and may be waiting for you to ask them if they would like to. Perhaps they are unsure what to do next. Offer to pray with them, and over a period of time help them to get involved in the journey of discipleship, as part of a bigger community of believers.

Community

As you saw in Study 7, being a part of the church is fundamental to being a Christian. We will not reiterate here the ideas about church discussed in that study. However, the fundamental point to make in the context of a discussion of mission is that the very existence of the church, as Christ's body on earth, is missional.

As the church lives in communion with God in the midst of a fallen world, it functions as a message of salvation. The relationships within the church, both between believers and between believers and God, are testimony to the power of the gospel. The triune God is a God of relationship—a divine community-in-being. If relationship is fundamental to the Godhead, then it must also be fundamental to God's people. As the church relates to God, in worship, prayer and through the sacraments, it testifies to what it means to live in communion with the living God.

> *the church is the mission*
>
> Lesslie Newbigin

ACTIVITY

Read Acts 2:41–47 and 4:32–35. Note that after responding to Peter's Pentecost sermon, the new believers' first act was to establish community. What did these believers share? What was their attitude?

If you can help a new believer become a part of a local church then you will be going a long way towards helping them become a disciple. But just attending church is not enough. The key is to become a part of the body of Christ, integrated into its fellowship and united with it in its service to God. The Christian church is a community that embodies an alternative set of values to those of the dominant society around it. The church provides the setting in which we try to build up the kingdom of God, at the same time engaged as salt and light in the world around us. The identity of the church, therefore, is missional: it is in the world but not of the world.

Service

Service is about demonstrating the gospel by serving the needs of others, modelled on Christ's service. As in Jesus' ministry, this service is relevant both for believers and for those who don't know Christ. By healing, feeding and protecting people, Jesus demonstrated the power of salvation to those around him. Likewise, our service should enact the message of salvation, so that others see the power of the gospel at work in the world.

Jesus calls upon his followers to be servants. This has to do with both attitude and action. To be a servant is to act in *humility* towards others, to seek God's glory rather than personal advancement in whatever you do. To be a servant also means *to serve,* to engage in works that live out the kingdom.

How do you demonstrate the message of salvation? By bringing God's presence into your community. Service is a manifestation of God's presence, and social action, from the church's perspective, is local mission. This means getting involved in the community. All churches have a role in their local community, whether they acknowledge it or not. The kind of testimony they provide to that community will depend on their involvement in it.

What should this service look like? Being a good neighbour is paramount. Jesus' parable of the Good Samaritan clarifies that your neighbour is anyone in need. As you saw at the beginning of this study, love for your neighbour means serving him or her as a whole person.

The church also serves God in the world by seeking the peace and good of the kingdom of God. Expressed conversely, the church is to resist evil, opposing anything that opposes the ethics of the kingdom. Just as Jesus set people free from demonic oppression, alleviated suffering and liberated people from the enslavement of sin, the church should likewise work against the forces of sin, death and destruction in the world. This may range from prayers for healing to feeding the homeless to political activism. The entire created order is God's: we need to live in a way that expresses God's ultimate sovereignty.

It is very easy to look at the destructive practices at loose in the world and to despair of ever making a difference. A wider, historical perspective helps here. The church has been enacting the kingdom throughout its history. When babies in first-century Greco-Roman society were exposed and left to die, the church rescued them. When barbaric European tribes were ravaging each other, the church established peace through the gospel. Hospitals, hospices, national education and the termination of the slave trade all have their roots in the church. Many other examples could be given.

ACTIVITY

Can you think of ways that you and your church might meet local needs as an act of service to the Creator God?

Some of these ideas will be taken further in Study 22 under 'social justice'.

The Gospel in Context

In this study you will consider some of the issues involved in living out the Christian faith within a particular context.

Bible passage: 1 Corinthians 9:19–27

STUDY QUESTIONS

What does this passage tell you about living out the gospel?

➢ What is Paul's driving goal in ministry? (vv.19 and 23)

➢ In vv.20–22, Paul gives 4 examples of adapting his behaviour. Based on this, how would you summarize Paul's mission strategy?

➢ Are there limits to this strategy?

➢ In vv.24–27, Paul uses an athletic metaphor to describe his approach. How does Paul attain his goal?

➢ Describe the lifestyle of an athlete in training. How are the disciplines of an athlete applicable to the Christian life?

➢ This passage is part of a wider argument Paul makes about giving up your rights, for the sake of the gospel. Yet Paul does not give up his rights as an end in itself. See Acts 22:25–29 or 25:9–12 for places where he asserts his rights, for the sake of the gospel. What are the implications of having the gospel as the overall paradigm guiding your life?

Three Contexts

Mission does not occur in a vacuum. It takes place in a constantly changing world that is neither historically nor culturally static. To engage in mission means to seek to communicate to this changing world in ways that can be understood.

Likewise, the church should not be static. Since the Spirit is continually at work transforming it, the church should be a developing organism, not an inert fixture. The church can and should adapt through historical and cultural changes, as the Spirit enables it to be Christ's body in its particular context.

How then does the church embody the gospel in different contexts? To answer this, at least three different cultural frameworks must be taken into account:

- the cultural world in which you live and work
- your personal faith and church tradition, which will significantly influence how you understand the gospel
- the cultural world of the Bible, which provides an alternative framework for viewing reality

We will consider each of these contexts before asking questions about how to bring them together. Drawing them together is called 'contextualizing' the gospel. To prevent the message of salvation from being held in cultural bondage to a particular era or cultural situation of the church, it is important to ask how the gospel speaks to the context you are in.

You and Your Church Tradition

We begin where you are. The first step in working out how to contextualize the gospel is personal self-awareness, particularly regarding how your church tradition shapes your faith. All of us are deeply influenced by our church tradition—whether by embracing it or reacting against it, or a bit of both. Everyone's perception of their faith is filtered through the tradition in which they worship and through which they receive theological teaching. Awareness of your theological background will help you to respond to that background in a mature way.

Much of this section will consist of activities aimed at helping you to think through what you believe and why you believe what you do.

ACTIVITY

Take a few minutes to list the church traditions to which you have been exposed and which have contributed to your understanding of your faith, whether positively or negatively.

ACTIVITY

Now write down, in short clear statements, your central Christian beliefs. It may help to think of this as a personal creed. Do not get caught up in details, but rather aim for main points.

ACTIVITY

Next think about how you express your faith. Make a list of the forms of worship, spirituality and Christian practice with which you are most comfortable and consider important to your faith.

How is it going so far? You should be building up a picture of your own faith. Try to be as honest as possible—the point of these exercises is to heighten your personal awareness, not to provide a perfect creedal statement, or to compare yourself to anyone else. The next set of exercises will make you think about where your beliefs have come from.

ACTIVITY

Choose the church tradition or traditions that you believe have had the most influence upon your personal faith. Take time out from this study to read about this tradition, or to talk to others about it. If you are doing this study in a group, your group should discuss the distinctives of your tradition. What is it, for instance, that sets you apart as Methodists or Baptists? Read the following two activities and keep these in mind as you have your discussion.

ACTIVITY

Which doctrines and practices of this tradition have you personally adopted? Why have you embraced each of these? Record a brief response to this question for each doctrine or practice.

ACTIVITY

Which doctrines and practices have you not adopted? Record briefly why you have rejected each of these.

It is important that your response to why you have embraced a particular belief or practice goes beyond 'because it's right'. Ask yourself why you believe it to be right. How do you know? Who told you and why do you believe them?

Not only your tradition but also your culture contribute significantly to what you believe. Your church is culturally conditioned, expressing its understanding of faith in and through a particular worldview that will shape what you believe. The cultural conditioning of our faith is evident when you gather together Christians from a variety of cultures. In the USA, for instance, many Christians believe that drinking wine in any form is sinful, while in Europe many Christians believe that moderate wine consumption is good for their health and enjoyable rather than sinful.

Your own faith will benefit greatly as you explore those things that have made their mark upon it.

ACTIVITY

Can you think of any cultural influences upon your own church or church tradition?

The Cultural World of the Bible

In order to express your faith effectively, not only do you need to take into account the influences of your own tradition, but also the distinct cultural world of Scripture. The biblical message is located in particular cultures and historical eras. Jesus, for example, lived and worked in first-century Palestine. The prophet Amos declared his oracles to the cultural and political situation of Israel in the eighth century BC. To understand the gospel message, how to express it as well as how to live it, you need to seek to understand the cultural world from which it emanates.

You have already covered much ground regarding the cultural world of the Bible in Units 3 and 4. We will not reiterate that here. Instead, we will simply emphasize that the Christian faith necessarily interprets the biblical message. Culture is the medium in which faith is expressed and lived out. Church traditions make sense of the gospel from the perspective of their historical era and cultural setting. This itself is a form of contextualization. It should come as no surprise that the Christian faith looks different in various cultural and historical contexts.

Baptism provides a useful example. While baptism has a clear biblical mandate, its form is less clear and practices regarding baptism have varied greatly through the centuries. Church traditions continue to debate whether or not the New Testament church baptized children or only adults—a debate that has never reached a conclusive answer. The Patristic church developed the practice of baptizing Gentile converts, of any age, after three years of catechism. The three years were deemed necessary to ensure that new believers understood the teaching of the church. A century or so later, the church in parts of the Roman Empire baptized believers on their deathbeds. They believed that Christians were forgiven only for the sins that occurred prior to baptism. In the medieval era, the church authorized midwives to baptize all newborn babies due to the high rate of infant mortality. Later, this practice was construed by both church and society as marking the entrance of the infant not only into the church, but into society in general (as in the practice of families with no interest in church still 'christening' their babies).

While your church tradition may look askance at some of these baptismal practices, the sheer variation in the interpretation of baptism through the centuries sounds a call for great humility. No doubt the church of the 22nd century will look back at some of our current church practices with dismay.

Your Culture

The third context you must take into account is your immediate cultural context. On a micro level, this could be your workplace, your local neighbourhood, or the community surrounding your church. On a macro level, this means the ethnic or national culture in which you live. Again, it is impossible for us to discuss here various cultures and sub-cultures in any detail. Instead, the focus here will be upon guiding you through a series of activities to help you probe this area a little more.

In order to be a part of God's mission in your local area or workplace, you need to have intimate knowledge of that place. For many of us, this is not difficult: it is normal to be immersed in our culture. Indeed many of us are so immersed that we find it difficult at times to see beyond the cultural framework in which we live. Attempting to describe what that context may look like to an outsider will help you to think through its characteristics.

ACTIVITY

First choose the context in which you or your church are living and working for God. This may be, for instance, your local community, your workplace, your village, or your town. Then, imagine that someone from a different country is visiting you and wants to understand how the people in your chosen place live, as well as why they live in the way that they do. How will you respond?

Next, consider the implications for serving God in your chosen community.

ACTIVITY

What challenges do the characteristics of your chosen community present to communicating and living out the biblical message?

You should also think about what would be good news for people in that context.

ACTIVITY

What are the needs of your chosen community? What kind of relationships do the people there have with one another? Looking at faith through their eyes, to what aspect of the gospel might they respond?

Working out appropriate ways in which to live out the gospel will depend, at least in part, upon the answers to these questions. How you can be salt and light in a community depends upon the nature of that community. Referring back to the previous study, how your church embodies the gospel, how you demonstrate the gospel and how you communicate it in a particular context depends to a large extent upon that context. To contextualize the gospel in your community, you must know and be a part of that community.

Contextualization

Contextualization may be defined as the process of making the Christian faith understandable in a particular cultural context. It involves adapting both yourself and your message to that culture, with the aim of enabling the people in that culture to respond meaningfully to the gospel. People should not have to change cultures in order to be Christians. Yes, the Christian church is counter-cultural and should never conform to what is fashionable. But to have a counter-cultural impact, the church must be a part of its community, not separatist. Withdrawal from the world around us rules out any attempt to be salt and light. If you gather all of the salt into the salt mill, it will never function as seasoning, but instead loses its purpose.

The 'seasoning' of the gospel is designed to transform culture. This means expressing faith through culture in a meaningful way. Think of Paul's strategy in 1 Corinthians 9—to those outside the law he became as one outside the law. Note that Paul doesn't himself become lawless (as he clarifies in v.21). Rather, he adapts his lifestyle to the people around him. In Corinth, Paul engaged in downward mobility for the sake of the gospel, working as a manual labourer instead of a paid preacher. Yet in adapting his behaviour, Paul does not compromise his faith. While he becomes weak to win the weak, he does not become a thief to win thieves. Paul's contextualization is morally neutral.

The two imperatives of contextualization are faithfulness to the biblical message and relevance to context. To be faithful to the biblical message means to ask what an expression of the gospel would look like in that cultural context—even if it is not a familiar expression in your own church's tradition. For the message to be relevant, it must be understood. Communicating through a mesh of spiritual jargon is like using a foreign language: it stereotypes you long before you can make yourself understood, erecting a barrier rather than dismantling one.

ACTIVITY

What language might you use to express the gospel in your chosen community?

As is evident from the 1 Corinthians 9 passage, living out the gospel does not involve a total rejection of local culture. Paul conformed to culture to the extent that it enabled him to be relevant. Yet Paul did not embrace all aspects of his context. Contextualization is also not about uncritical acceptance of culture.

Contextualization is an approach to the gospel that seeks to avoid irrelevance on the one hand, and wholesale cultural accommodation on the other. Accommodation is the error of too much relevance: the church following the values of the world around it. Irrelevance is the rejection of the culture of the world around to the extent that the gospel message can no longer be heard clearly.

Instead, contextualization is about the gospel transforming culture. At times this will mean tension: the gospel will often look foolish to those who don't understand it and the cross is certainly counter-cultural (1 Corinthians 1:18–25). Those who choose to live in poor inner city areas for the sake of the gospel will look foolish in a success-obsessed culture. Transformation involves change, and change is rarely painless.

ACTIVITY

Spend some time considering how to contextualize the gospel in your chosen community. What will this mean for your lifestyle? For your church? How can you avoid irrelevance or accommodation?

The Uniqueness of Jesus

We conclude our unit on mission with a discussion of the uniqueness of Christ in relation to other world religions.

Bible passage: 2 Corinthians 5:11–21

STUDY QUESTIONS

What do you learn from this passage about involvement in mission?

- ➤ To whom is Paul accountable and how does this impact his ministry? (vv.11–13)
- ➤ For whom did Christ die and what are the implications?
- ➤ How should Jesus' death alter our perspective on others? (v.16)
- ➤ How does being in Jesus fundamentally alter humanity? (v.17)
- ➤ How does the passage describe God's reconciliation of the world?
- ➤ What are the responsibilities of ambassadors for Christ?
- ➤ What motivates Paul? What motivates you?

Introduction

Christianity is a faith caught between the first and second comings of Jesus. We see signs of the kingdom in our lives, and yet we also see evidence of the old order: sin, disease and death. Suffering is not only physical but manifest in every aspect of our existence: broken relationships, meaninglessness, despair, apathy. People seek relief from the old order in all sorts of ways: through science, spiritual healing, psychotherapy, religious practice, addictive behaviour and economic advancement, to name just a few.

Into the darkness of this old order, the Christian faith shines a light of hope. But then, it could be argued, so do other religions. Most of them bring a sense of meaning to life, as well as providing moral guidance. Almost all religions have a sacred book, major figures whose teachings are greatly respected, and traditions that are passed down by believers. Many religious adherents talk about a sense of belonging to their own group, including their own 'testimonies' of people joining them. What then, if anything, makes Christianity more than just another religion?

Jesus

What makes Christianity different is Jesus. Christianity stands out not just because of Jesus' teaching and example, but because of who Jesus was. Jesus' own understanding of his uniqueness is expressed radically in John's gospel: 'I am the way and the truth and the life. No one comes to the Father except through me' (John 14:6). At the heart of this statement is Jesus' unique provision of salvation for humanity.

While you may find comparable moral guidelines in other religions, this is not the same as saying that the Christian concept of salvation can be found in other religions. Other religious systems do have their own understanding of salvation—the Buddhist concept of *nirvana* (a state of perfect peace or 'deathlessness') provides a good example. But none have a divine saviour who self-sacrificially reconciles humanity to God, leading to human transformation and eternal life.

In Romans 1 to 8, Paul argues that sin is a universal problem for humanity, in response to which Jesus' death acts as a 'sin offering' or atonement, bringing a release from sin. The universal problem has one single universal solution. Romans 5:18–19 is a particularly clear statement of this. As you saw in the 2 Corinthians passage at the beginning of this study, Christ is central to God's reconciliation of the world to himself.

We have already examined salvation in Study 6. The aim here is not to discuss that material again, but rather to emphasize its uniqueness within the Christian faith. The early church was well aware of the revolutionary nature of Jesus' death and resurrection, and proclaimed it boldly.

ACTIVITY

How does Peter express the uniqueness of Jesus' salvation in Acts 4:12? You may find it useful to read 4:1–12, to understand the verse in its context. Peter and John have just healed a lame man.

When we discuss the 'uniqueness of Christ' we therefore have two things in view: the unique way of salvation that is through Christ, and the uniqueness of who Christ was. Unlike any other teacher Christ did not just point the way to God; he was unique because the fullness of deity lived in bodily form in him (Colossians 2:9). No other great religious teacher has ever claimed to be God come to earth for the sake of human salvation.

Christianity and other Religions

Religion is notoriously difficult to define. Is it a belief system? Does this then open the door to ideologies such as Marxism, secular humanism and hedonism? Or must it include ritual, sacred texts or a deity? What then of New Age spirituality or even Buddhism, which is not theistic? If worship is essential to the definition, then devotion to a local football team may be a religion (indeed for some people it is!).

But however we define religion, the fact is that human beings are religious creatures. We all operate under a belief system, even if an unacknowledged one. We seek meaning and purpose in life. We want justice, we know the value of power and we worship, in obvious or in subtle ways, whatever we think controls our destiny—whether money, science, our ancestors or God. Direction in life and moral guidance are rooted in this worship.

Religion has to do with the framing of reality. People from different religious persuasions interpret reality in different ways. Your religious faith explains the significance of your life and how the world works. Building on this, religious belief guides conduct, indicating how to live in view of its particular framing of reality.

ACTIVITY

Based on the above discussion, in what ways is Christianity a religion?

Christianity provides a clear framework through which its adherents view reality, including God as creator, a fallen world and redemption in Christ. Scripture abounds with ethical precepts for the guidance of life in relation to God. Christians gain both meaning and purpose in life through their relationship with their Saviour.

What then should we make of the biblical view of religious practices? In the Torah—the first five books of the Old Testament—God gives his people, the Israelites, a set of laws for life in relation to him. This includes detailed instruction for specific forms of religious practice. How does this fit with other emphases later in the Bible?

ACTIVITY

Read Amos 5:21–27. How does God evaluate the Israelites' worship here? What is the reason for this divine displeasure? (v.24) How should we read v.25? Another passage with a similar balance between justice and religion is Isaiah 1, see especially vv.12–17.

The prophets critique religious practice only when it takes the place of the fundamental requirements of justice and righteousness. A famous summary of this prophetic teaching is Micah 6:8. When we read Amos 5 it almost seems to suggest that even in the days of Moses Israel did not offer sacrifices (v.25): probably we should read this as saying 'Is this (the current way you are behaving) what you were doing when you worshipped me in the desert?'. At the risk of over-simplification, the Old Testament always assumes that the religious practices God requires flow out from the heart of the relationship between God and his people, and do not constitute that relationship. The problem in Isaiah 1, in other words, is hypocrisy: worshipping with rituals while living a life that denies their significance.

ACTIVITY

Read Matthew 23:1–36. In what ways are the Pharisees also religious but hypocritical? How is Jesus' call to humility, in vv.8–12, an antidote to this?

Any ritual that is performed for the sake of being seen by others is self-seeking rather than God-seeking. The Pharisees were devoted to Scripture—they were the biblical scholars of their day—but their attitudes were wrong.

Applying these thoughts to religions outside of the Judaeo-Christian tradition, religious practice as a human construct cannot enable people to meet with God. Religious systems, which produce a human interpretation of existence removed from God's revelation of reality, will invariably mislead. As long as secular humanists, for instance, believe that humanity is the ultimate power on earth, they will continue to misinterpret the human predicament.

Many other religious faiths, of course, believe in a divine being or beings. But are they the same deities? (Recall our look at the identity of Yhwh in Study 1). This raises the question: are all religions fundamentally the same? To embrace this position, that all religions are the same, is to embrace Hinduism, which asserts that all religious paths ultimately lead to God. Yet Hinduism advocates neither a creator nor judgement but has many gods, while Buddhism is godless, agnostic Confucianism interprets god as 'the ultimate moral principle', and Islam insists that Allah's monotheism is undifferentiated (i.e., not trinitarian) and his control over human life authoritarian. In short, there is no evidence that the deities of all the major religions are in fact the same one, and most of the religions explicitly deny this. Such a view can only be maintained by ignoring the religious traditions themselves.

If all religions are not the same, then we are left with two options. Either they are all wrong, or only one of them is right. To assert that they are all wrong leads, invariably, to the construction of a belief system of humanity's own making. This is the path taken by those atheists who believe that by ridding the world of god, they have made it a better place. But god is then replaced by money, science or a political system, and humanity finds itself bowing to idols of its own making. The evidence of the last century is not encouraging for atheism: violence, injustice and totalitarianism have never been far away from atheist political regimes.

This leaves the final option: that one faith has it right. This should not, however, lead to intolerance between religious traditions. Many have helpful ethical principles from which all may benefit, even if one does not agree with their interpretation of reality. From a Christian perspective, tolerance is not about agreeing with the tenets of other faiths so much as treating their adherents with respect and accepting them in Christ's love. The Christian claim to have found the right way to God should be a respectful claim offered in humility to others, rather than imposed on them.

ACTIVITY

Compare Christianity to another religious faith. Choose one with which you have some familiarity, or take time to research one. How are they similar? How are they different? What can you learn from the other faith?

What About Those Who Have Never Heard?

A problem with this position on the uniqueness of Christ is that it can be easier to state in theory than to defend in practice. Many missionaries have had doubts when confronted with people in other cultures and religions, who appear to be leading lives characterized by qualities of a Christian life. The position is further complicated when such people, upon hearing the gospel, respond to it positively almost as if it is, for them, a better way of expressing what they have believed all along. Does God, through natural revelation and the power of his Holy Spirit, work in places where the gospel is not yet known? Can people who have never heard the gospel receive salvation?

The difficult question of the plight of those who have never heard the gospel has been debated passionately for many centuries. Before looking at the debate, we should underline carefully something upon which most Christians may agree. When people are saved it is through the unique work of Jesus Christ on the cross and in the resurrection. This is not, at least in our discussion, a matter for debate. The issue here is rather: how much does someone actually need to be aware of in order to be saved?

A variety of different answers to this question are summarized next[11] (with possible biblical support or examples):

---

[11] Adapted from John Sanders, ed., *What About Those Who Have Never Heard?* (Downers Grove: IVP, 1995) p.20

Restrictivism	God does not provide salvation to those who fail to hear of Jesus and come to faith in him before they die (John 3:17–21, 1 John 5:10–12)
Universal Opportunity Before Death	All people are given opportunity to be saved by God sending the gospel (for instance by angels or dreams) before death (examples in Daniel 2, Acts 8)
Inclusivism	The unevangelized may be saved if they respond in faith to God based on the revelation they have (John 12:27–32, Acts 10:1–8,34–48, 1 Timothy 4:10, Hebrews 11:6)
Divine Perseverance (or Postmortem Evangelism)	The unevangelized receive an opportunity to believe in Jesus after death (1 Peter 3:18–4:6)
Universalism	All people will in fact be saved by Jesus. No one is damned for ever. (Romans 5:18, 1 John 2:2)

Figure 4

ACTIVITY

Look up the biblical references for each of the positions listed in Figure 4, seeking to understand how each position may be defended. If you are working in a group, divide the positions among you and then present your findings to each other.

Both inclusivism and universalism assert that people may be saved through the death and resurrection of Jesus even if they have never heard of him. Such people obviously do not profess to be Christians and may belong to other religions.

Comparing two of the positions may help you to think about them more clearly. Inclusivism accepts what appears to be true: that some have a faith in Christ without knowing it. This honours peoples' sincerity in their search for God, while holding to the belief that if anyone is saved, it is through Christ. It tries to do justice to a certain strand of biblical thinking, namely that Christ is the true light who has come to every human being (e.g. John

1:9), even if they cannot attach an accurate name to that light. Inclusivism believes that all truth is God's truth.

Restrictivism, in contrast, accepts the real nature of spiritual conflict in different religions, and the power of worshipping false gods. Being a good person is not the same as being a Christian. Can we really call someone a Christian if they do not profess Christ? This position tries to do justice to a certain strand of biblical thinking, namely that mission is an essential part of taking Christ to those who are lost without him.

You may be wondering what motivates those who hold an inclusivist position to engage in mission? Inclusivists point out that knowing Jesus brings the light of eternal life into people's lives. Those who have only a weak or minimal understanding of that light—for example, those who have never heard the gospel but may have some understanding of God through natural revelation—will go through this life in semi-darkness, groping after the small light that they have. Introducing them to Jesus is tantamount to switching from a spluttering match to a powerful floodlight.

God's mission is to bring the full light of understanding to all people, to make a difference in their lives both for now and on into eternity.

ACTIVITY

Which of the five positions do you think is most helpful and why? What implications does your position hold for your participation in God's mission to the world?

UNIT VI—CHRISTIAN HOPE

Our citizenship is in heaven,
and it is from there that we are
expecting a Saviour,
the Lord Jesus Christ.
He will transform our humble
bodies
that they may be conformed to the
body of his glory,
by the power that also enables him
to make all things subject to himself.

Philippians 3:20–21

This final unit leads you to focus forward, to consider the hope of the Christian life, and its power to equip and guide you in your daily life. By looking forward, we gain guidance for how to walk and which direction to take on our current path. It is hope that inspires, motivates and enables us as we seek to be God's people wherever he has placed us.

STUDIES

21 Hope for the Individual
22 Hope for the World
23 Hope for the Future
24 Living with Hope

Hope for the Individual

In this study we look at Christian hope as it impacts the individual believer: the hope of resurrection and eternal life, and the difference that this hope makes to us already in this life.

Bible Passage: 1 Corinthians 15:35–58

STUDY QUESTIONS

What does this passage say about the resurrection of believers?

➢ What questions about the resurrection body does Paul anticipate? (v.35)

➢ Paul uses three analogies to explain the nature of our resurrection bodies. What is the point of each? (vv.36–38, 39–44a, 44b–49)

➢ What is the point of v.50?

➢ What does Paul say happens to death? (vv.54–57)

➢ What should be our response? (v.58)

Life Abundant and Eternal

In a memorable passage in John's gospel, Jesus says that he is the 'good shepherd' who has come so that we 'may have life, and have it abundantly' (or 'in all its fullness')—John 10:10. The strong focus in the Bible is on life as we live it with God, here and now, and only secondarily on life after death. However, the way the New Testament sees it, one of the reasons we are confident about life here and now is that we have a hope about life after death.

Many of the ways we talk about 'life after death' in Christianity do not match up very closely to the way the New Testament speaks, as we shall see throughout this unit. An interesting example of this is the way John's gospel speaks about 'eternal life'.

ACTIVITY

Read John 3:15 (as well as 3:16, a more famous verse). What is the significance of the present tense in this verse: when do believers have eternal life? Read also John 11:25 and 8:51.

John has Jesus saying that if we believe in him, we have eternal life—in other words, we already have it, now. When Jesus describes himself as 'the resurrection', in John 11:25, he suggests that this life we have with him is so powerful that it will not be disrupted by death.

The phrase translated 'eternal life' in John's gospel (and in fact throughout the New Testament) is *zōē aiōnios,* which we could literally translate as 'life of the ages'. It is 'eternal' because these 'ages' are everlasting, but perhaps even more significantly, it is a life characterized with the quality of being with God for ever. 'Eternal life', then, is not only a life without end, but it is a life that is filled (already) with the fullness of God, who is Lord of all time. John 10:10 is talking about eternal life when it says 'life in all its fullness'. This should remind you of our discussion of the 'kingdom of God' in Study 11. This life with God is already begun, even though it is not yet fully experienced in our world.

ACTIVITY

When we think of Christian hope, do we think primarily of the future or the world around us?

In an important sense, the biblical answer to this question is that it is not the right question. The future is already begun with the resurrection of Jesus, and we already live in God's (eternal) kingdom. So our hope is future, but it is already present. As Paul writes to the Colossians, God has chosen to make known 'the riches of the glory of this mystery, which is Christ in you, the hope of glory' (Colossians 1:27).

ACTIVITY

When we think about the death of a Christian whom we know well, how do we understand the tension between the sense of loss (or grief) on the one hand, and the sense that they have moved on to be with God on the other? Does it differ depending on the age of the person who died or the circumstances of their death?

Responding to Death

The Bible makes it clear, indeed it simply assumes, that physical death is not the end. Earthly life is not the sum total of a human's existence. Physical death marks an obvious kind of end, and erects a boundary beyond which empirical research cannot go. It leads to separation from those who are known and loved. It is clearly, in this sense, an enemy to humanity. The pain, grief and loss it causes can be devastating. Even for those who know that their deceased loved one is safe in God's presence, the loss in this life is painful and real, and should be neither ignored nor treated lightly. This is especially so with those who do not die 'old and full of years', as the Bible describes people like Abraham (Genesis 25:8). The Bible recognizes the difference between what it calls a 'natural death' (e.g. Numbers 16:29) and death as a violent interruption of human life, as when Jeremiah describes it as an intruder breaking in through the windows (Jeremiah 9:21).

The biblical view of death encompasses but is also more than the ending of physical life. Disobedience in the Garden of Eden leads to separation. Death means alienation from God and other people during earthly existence, culminating in physical separation at the end of this existence. Ultimate death is permanent separation from God. The response to death is not to hope for some disembodied post-death existence, but is to set out along the path marked by Jesus' death and resurrection. Although this path still leads—for the time being—through death, it comes out the other side into a new, transformed eternal life.

> *All birth was but the*
> *prelude unto death*
> *And every cradle*
> *swung above a grave.*
> *The sun made weary*
> *trips from east to west,*
> *Time found no shore,*
> *and culture screamed*
> *and raved.*
>
> *The world, in peaceless*
> *orbits, sped along*
> *And waited for the*
> *Singer and his song.*
>
> Calvin Miller[12]

---

[12] *The Singer* (Downers Grove: IVP, 1975) p.40

Transformed Bodies

In 1 Corinthians 15, Paul envisages the transformation of each believer through resurrection. He is responding to the Corinthians' misconceptions about resurrection. They seemed to have believed that at death, their spirits cast off their physical bodies and that their eternal existence would be that of a disembodied spirit. To this Paul replies: no, no, no. He begins chapter 15 by patiently explaining to the Corinthians the necessity of Jesus' bodily resurrection for the salvation of the whole created order (see Study 6). He then goes on to discuss the physical transformation that takes place in resurrection.

The Corinthians could not grasp how their physical bodies could be raised to life. Would those who died as children have the same kind of bodies as those who died in old age? What about those who had lost limbs in a car crash (or, to avoid anachronism, a chariot race)? Paul responds 'how foolish!' (v.36): you are thinking about this all wrong. He then corrects their thinking using three analogies.

ACTIVITY

What is the relationship between a seed and the plant it produces? How are they different and how are they the same? If possible, hold a tree seed in your palm—for example an apple seed—and compare it to the tree it could potentially produce.

How can your body be eternal? It is the seed. Just as a tiny apple seed turns into a tall tree, so your body will be transformed into a new, magnificent form. You cannot conceive of your resurrection body by looking at your current body. Just as the appearance of the seed doesn't reveal the final form of the plant, neither does your current body indicate its resurrection form.

And yet there is continuity between the seed and the plant it becomes. The plant cannot exist without the seed and, somehow, the plant is the seed in a new state of being. Likewise, there will be continuity between your current body and your resurrection body. In fact, continuity between your current existence and your future existence is provided by your body. Now you have a physical body, then you will have what Paul calls a 'spiritual' body. But the way to understand this is that the body you will have is *pneumatikos*—'of the spirit'. In other words, it is still a body (belonging to and characterized by the Spirit). Paul has no concept of continuing to exist as a disembodied spirit.

To produce the tree, the seed must be buried and die. Its death allows transformation. Through his resurrection, Jesus did not reverse death— he too died—but he made a path through it. In John 12:24 Jesus states, 'unless a grain of wheat falls into the earth and dies, it remains just a single seed. But if it dies, it bears much fruit.' Jesus is referring to his own death, which enables others to have life.

Our physical bodies must undergo a transformation, and for most of us, death is the path to that transformation. Paul's point in 1 Corinthians 15:50 is that change is a necessity. Although not everyone will die (v.51)—here Paul is referring to the believers who are alive at Christ's return—everyone must be transformed in order to live in God's presence.

ACTIVITY

Think for a few moments about how different creatures have bodies that are adapted to their environment. Fish, for example, have fins to swim, while camels have water storage compartments on their backs that enable them to survive in the desert. What might this tell you about the kind of body you will have in the kingdom?

Paul goes on in vv.39–41 to indicate that God has given each of his creations a body that is adapted to its environment—not only people but also animals, birds, fish, and even the planets and stars. Each order of existence has its own corresponding body. If God can create such diverse orders of being, he can make for you a spiritual body that is adapted to life in his kingdom. You cannot guess the form and shape of that new body based on your current life, but we can say that since the new order of existence will be glorious, so will your body be. As Paul indicates in vv.42–44, your resurrection body will be 'imperishable', raised in glory and power.

ACTIVITY

What was Jesus' resurrection body like? You may find it useful to look at John 20:10–29 and Luke 24:13–42.

Through his seed analogy, Paul stresses the continuity between our current physical bodies and our transformed spiritual bodies. But in vv.44b–49, he foregrounds the discontinuity between the two bodies through his discussion of the difference between Adam and Christ. Adam and the resurrected Christ represent the two types of bodily existence, and the contrast between them highlights the difference between earthly and kingdom existence.

The natural or physical body is made from the earth and for the earth. It is a part of the created order. Being descendants of the human race, we all receive bodies like Adam at birth. He was mortal, and so are we. His body was subject to sin, death and decay, and so are ours. Your current body is an Adam-body, created good but marred by sin, yet still potentially reflecting the image of God.

Christ, the second Adam, through his death and resurrection is freed from the problems of the physical body. Jesus' resurrection defeats the power that sin and death have over the created order (see Study 6). Christ's resurrection body is a spiritual body that has been transformed through the power of God. As we have already emphasized, the spiritual body is an actual body, giving the sin-free human spirit form and shape. Christ's body is from heaven; it is immortal. And you will receive a body like his. In the resurrected Jesus, we see humanity in its exalted form.

Why, then, does the Spirit take up residence in our Adam bodies? The Holy Spirit prepares us for our future spiritual bodies. The Spirit has already begun the process of transforming you to be like Christ, a transformation that will only come to full fruition in the kingdom. Now you are at an in between stage. You are a new creation—the Spirit has germinated new life within you. Yet you must still battle the sinful nature that is a part of your earthly body. As Paul describes in Romans 8:23, we have 'the first fruits of the Spirit', yet also 'groan inwardly while we wait for our adoption, the redemption of our bodies'.

ACTIVITY

Pause for a moment to reflect upon how the Spirit is transforming you.

The Defeat of Death

1 Corinthians 15:26 indicates that death is the final enemy to be destroyed, and death's ultimate defeat occurs at the resurrection of believers, God's surprising and wonderful twist in the drama of salvation. Death is swallowed up for ever (Isaiah 25:7) through resurrection. Paul concludes his argument in vv.54–57 by returning to this topic of the defeat of death.

The taunting questions aimed at death are taken from Hosea 13:14. What is death's victory? It is power over humanity, which is abolished by the resurrection. What is death's sting? It is sin, the poison that leads to death: once you are stung by sin, death is inevitable. Death comes into the world through sin, so the defeat of death occurs through the defeat of sin, highlighting the profound connection between Jesus' death and resurrection.

While physical death in this world leads to separation from loved ones, ultimate death is separation from God. To be for ever separated from God's love is to cease to live. Physical death, having been defeated by the resurrection, is at the end cast into a 'lake of fire' (see Revelation 20:13–14).

An Eternal Perspective

Our response to this victory is summed up in 1 Corinthians 15:58, where Paul calls upon his readers to live and work for the Lord since their lives have eternal significance. This makes it clear that Christian hope is not a hope to be released from this life but a hope for the future that already transforms this present life. If our bodies count for eternity, then we are encouraged to make them count for the present. Paul makes a similar point in 2 Corinthians 5:1–10. Christ's resurrection contains our future and should shape our present.

Verse 58 also emphasizes the confidence of Christian hope: 'you know that in the Lord your labour is not in vain.' For those who place their hope in God's ultimate redemption of this world, life has both a future orientation and great day-to-day significance.

ACTIVITY

In what do you place your hope and how does it influence your daily life? How has this study of resurrection hope helped you to see things differently?

Eternal life begins now. Through the Holy Spirit, believers have a foretaste—albeit sometimes a weak one—of the resurrection life. This hope spills over into the world around us. The resurrection ties together creation and redemption: God's good creation, currently in bondage to decay, is set free by the triumph of life over death (see Romans 8:19–23). The created order is not rejected but redeemed. The result is renewal, a new heaven and a new earth in which God dwells with his people, a new order of existence for all.

Hope blends expectation with confidence. For the individual, expectation of a transformed life in God's new order gives confidence to be God's child in the current world. It is to this world that we turn next.

Hope for the World

What is the importance of faith to the world around us? Even a small candle changes the conditions in a large room. Think then of how the potency of the gospel impacts life around it, as it exposes darkness and expresses the power of light.

Bible Passages: Amos 5:4–24 and Matthew 5:1–48

STUDY QUESTIONS

What does the Amos passage tell you about God's view of justice? (Note that we also looked at the Amos passage, from a different perspective, in Study 20.)

> ➤ What conduct is Amos rebuking? How will God punish this conduct?
> ➤ What does God want the Israelites to pursue instead?
> ➤ In vv.21–24, what does God desire instead of worship?
> ➤ In the Matthew passage, what do you learn about living out faith?
> ➤ Which groups of people are called blessed? (vv.3–12)
> ➤ What do the two analogies in vv.13–14 indicate about a Christian's relationship to the world?
> ➤ In vv.17–18, Jesus indicates that he fulfils the Old Testament law and prophets. Which specific commandments does he mention in vs.21–48?
> ➤ How does Jesus interpret each of these commandments?

Shaping the Present

As you saw in the previous study, Christian faith is expectant. This expectancy is for the final victory of God, not only in individual lives but also in the world. The Christian faith hopes for victory over all of the forces of sin and death. Among those forces are pain, injustice, war and broken relationships, in fact anything that tears apart or destroys God's created order. The gospel works against these forces of destruction. It is like a yeast that spreads peace, justice, love and reconciliation. Where the gospel is, there should be signs of the kingdom.

Hope is not merely optimism. It is not about finding something positive to say in the face of a disaster or tragedy. Nor is it about writing off this world and living only for the next, as if this life were just a rehearsal for what really matters. Salvation is for life now, as well as for the future. True hope shares in the pain of this world and points to an alternative way of life characterized by the good of the gospel. Hope shapes the present while looking to the future, in the light of the God we have known in the past.

ACTIVITY

How do you define hope? In what forms do you detect its presence—or absence—in the world around you?

Stewards of Creation

The universe from its inception was good. Human beings, the climax of creation, were called upon by God to 'be fruitful and increase in number; fill the earth and subdue it' and to rule over the animals and use nature for food (Genesis 1:28–30). Although some have taken the injunction to rule and subdue as an excuse for domination, these instructions in fact point to human responsibility. As the bearers of God's image, human beings are to care for, nurture and develop creation in the same way that God cares for humanity. And God's care for humanity led to his self-sacrificial death on the cross: note that Paul talks about all of creation in Romans 8:18–25, not just about human beings.

ACTIVITY

Look at some of ways in which human beings interact with all of creation in Genesis 1–11 (in addition to 1:28–30 looked at above). For example:

—Genesis 2:15—what is the man's work?

—Genesis 3:17–18—what will be the nature of the relationship after 'the fall'?

—Genesis 8:1—who or what is included in what 'God remembers' during the flood? (note also 6:19)

—Genesis 9:1–17—read through this passage and look for ways that God is committing both to humans and other aspects of the creation.

Genesis 1–11 is a key passage for understanding God's care for creation because it is the part of Scripture that occurs before the focus on a 'chosen people'—the story of Israel. As a scene-setting for this longer story, the basic framework is set up where humanity and the animal and plant creation together occupy the planet in what should be a harmonious and productive environment. It is interesting to note that in Genesis 11 the humans set themselves to build a tower 'with its top in the heavens' (Babel—11:4) in direct opposition to the divine command to fill the earth (as noted above and in Genesis 9:1). When humans look out for themselves, Genesis 11 seems to say, it is a failure to take seriously their role as stewards of God's creation.

ACTIVITY

In the light of Genesis 1–11 (and especially 1:28–30 and chapter 9), how should humans understand their role as stewards of creation? In what ways has humanity been a threat to aspects of creation? How can humanity be a blessing to creation? For examples of specific questions, consider:

—Do these chapters encourage us in any way to think of being vegetarians?

—Are there implications for the ways we should interpret weather patterns, such as, perhaps, the effects of global warming?

—How do you care for your environment or make a difference in your area in the use of natural resources?

Christian Ethics

Working out how to live in this world is a matter of ethics. Ethics is the process of making moral decisions in any given situation. Christian ethics seeks to anchor this morality in God. How does a life of faith express itself in any given situation? Ethics has to do with how we live: how we decide whether an action is right or wrong. It also has to do with values: how and why we evaluate something as good or bad.

To seek to be God's people is to seek to be holy, and in the Bible a key result of holiness is commitment to living a life of ethical integrity. Israel was called to be ethically distinct from the nations around it. This is a constant theme of Deuteronomy (for example 7:1–6, 8:19–20, 12:4). Christians are equally called to be ethically distinct from those around them. The passage in Matthew that you explored at the beginning of this study is the first part of Jesus' 'Sermon on the Mount', found in Matthew 5–7. This sermon epitomizes Christian ethics, providing a manifesto for the life of God's kingdom in the midst of the world.

Perhaps few aspects of Christianity are more demanding than this: living as people of integrity in a crooked world, or as Paul puts it, shining like stars 'in the midst of a crooked and perverse generation' (Philippians 2:15). But equally, few are as important. Everything we do in response to God's salvation involves ethical judgements. Ethical integrity is central to being God's people. It is about being salt and light to those around us.

ACTIVITY

List a few ethical issues faced by Christians. How do you respond to these issues? What process do you use? If working in a group, get everyone to think through a different issue.

Making ethical decisions is by no means always straightforward. A simple example is found in the sixth of the ten commandments in Exodus 20:13: 'you shall not murder' (also traditionally translated as 'you shall not kill'). Indeed the decision about how to translate this verse already involves judgements about what kinds of killing count as murder. Scripture is full of examples of the dire consequences of killing (for example, Cain's killing of Abel in Genesis 4:1–16 or David's arrangements for the death of Uriah in 2 Samuel 11:1 –12:19). But if killing is always wrong, then why does the

Mosaic law contain guidelines for stoning to death anyone who sacrifices a child to a foreign idol? Or putting to death all witches and wizards—not to mention anyone who curses their father or mother (Leviticus 20:1–5,9,27)? Perhaps we are allowed to kill the wicked? In addition to all of these examples, there is the topic of 'holy war': where Israel was commanded to wipe out its enemies when it entered the land (as, e.g., in Deuteronomy 7:1–6).

The sixth commandment is probably focused on cases of killing outside of the remit of the law or the state. This does not resolve the question of whether or not Christians can be entitled to kill, it simply points out that this particular commandment, like most of the ten in fact, is not a word for all times and places, but had a particular function at the time it was given.

For someone standing in the 21st century and looking back, Old Testament laws may look out-dated and irrelevant, but rather than overthrowing the sixth commandment, Jesus builds on it, teaching that even being angry with and insulting another person is wrong (Matthew 5:21–22). Should all Christians be pacifists? The basic ethical issues concern our understanding of the value of human life and whether (or in what circumstances) it could be right to end life.

Ethical decisions are also impacted by circumstances. Life during wartime, for example, often seems to require different evaluations of what to do. A striking example of this occurred with those who helped to hide Jewish people in Nazi-occupied Europe in 1940. Confronted with a Nazi official knocking at the door and asking whether you knew of the location of this Jew, it seemed obvious that the 'right' response was to lie. How does such a situation help us to reflect upon the applicability of the commandment to tell the truth? This example is very close to a biblical one.

ACTIVITY

Read Joshua 2:1–14 to see how Rahab lies to protect the Israelite spies. How is this act described in Hebrews 11:31? What are the ethical implications?

Of course, God's commands do not result from arbitrary divine decisions. Rather, they are founded on God's nature and provide guidance for human beings to live in light of that nature. We make ethical decisions guided by God's moral character. The command not to kill could be said to derive from an understanding of God as a loving creator of all people, not just 'people like us'. This is a love that Christians are called upon to imitate and live out. Is it ever possible to hold together 'loving your neighbour as yourself' and killing?

Jesus in fact sums up the law in the two greatest commandments: loving God and loving others (Matthew 22:36–40). And here lies the crux of Christian ethics: it prioritizes God and others. While some forms of ethics place either the individual or the individual's family or country at their centre, making decisions and determining values based upon what is best for that individual or that family/people group/country, Christian ethics places God at the centre, and others on a level with yourself.

ACTIVITY

Read Matthew 22:36–40. Note that the second commandment calls upon you to love your neighbour *as* yourself. How does this differ from loving your neighbour *more* than yourself? What are the implications? You may want to compare this to Matthew 7:12.

Social Justice

Although the church is conceived of as counter-cultural, providing an alternative set of values to secular and pagan society, it is also called to be the salt and light that permeate and alter that society. The church not only demonstrates an alternative framework for living, it also works to enable others to benefit from that framework.

ACTIVITY

Consider for a moment how salt and light work to alter their contexts. What does this indicate about the work of the church?

A particular, and important, area in which the church works ethically is social justice; that is, the enactment of justice in the structures of society. As you saw in the Amos passage, God sets himself against systems that oppress people. Courts and legal systems that mete out injustice rather than justice are offensive. Lifestyles that promote wealth at the expense of others' poverty are unacceptable. Seeing others in need and ignoring them betrays a lack of love (see 1 John 3:17).

Justice has to do with fair conduct and treatment, and the biblical litmus test for justice is often treatment of the poor and marginalized. The Old Testament prophets emphasize that God is on the side of the oppressed. In the Amos passage, Israel stands condemned before God for its treatment of the poor. No amount of worship and sacrifice can atone for the hypocrisy of injustice, particularly when that injustice occurs alongside the regular practices of worship.

ACTIVITY

How might the Amos 5 passage be applicable to the relationship between the West and the developing world?

The New Testament widens this portrait. Jesus' mission statement in Luke 4:18–19 declares his intent to liberate the oppressed (see Study 18). Jesus' ministry enacts these words as he cares holistically for people, restoring sight to the blind, healing the sick, exorcizing demons and preaching salvation. He demonstrates interest in the current lives of people and alleviates their suffering in the present. Compassion and justice drive the attention he gives to the socially powerless, such as the chronically ill, social outcasts and widows.

> *When those who wield economic power are out of control, and serve their own interests to the detriment of the masses, the poor, and the powerless, Christians must speak prophetically and pronounce God's judgement against such destructive self-interest.*
>
> Tony Campolo[13]

Following Jesus' model, one of the early church's first acts was to organize distribution of food to widows (Acts 6:1–6; see also James 1:27 and 1 Timothy 5:3–10). To be a model of God's kingdom—even if an imperfect one—the church needs to be a force for justice in the world, working against institutionalized evil and seeking the peace of the gospel.

ACTIVITY

---

[13] *Adventures in Missing the Point: How the Culture-Controlled Church Neutered the Gospel* (Grand Rapids: Zondervan, 2003) p.108

The 'Fair Trade' movement seeks to achieve fairer economic distribution between countries. How might this impact the place where you live? Are there practical local ways where you can make a difference internationally?

Injustice arises not only from individual conduct but also from economic and legal structures. Economic systems and trade laws that advantage Western corporations and disadvantage the developing world perpetuate injustice. Arguably the current state of global economic disequilibrium amounts to economic slavery for the developing world.

'Liberation theology' is a way of thinking theologically that specifically addresses such structures, aligning itself with the plight of the poor and marginalized. Recognizing that theology, in any form, may be used to support and even to justify existing power structures, adherents of liberation theology seek to use theology for the benefit of the oppressed. It is thus a branch of theology that focuses upon *doing*—always informed by reflection upon the plight of humanity. The suffering of the poor, according to liberation theology, is a prophetic cry against injustice.

When people say that politics and religion do not mix, I wonder which Bible they have been reading.

Desmond Tutu

Hope for the Future

We turn now to the future. In Study 21, you considered the future transformation of the individual believer. Here we look at the future of the people of God and of the world.

Bible Passage: Revelation 20:1 – 22:6

STUDY QUESTIONS

How does the Revelation passage depict God's new world?

> The era described in 20:1–6 is known as the 'millennium'. What is the main point of this passage in relation to the current world order?

> In 20:11–15, who is judged and how?

> Make a list of things from the current order that the new heaven and new earth will exclude.

> Make a list of things that will be included.

> In what ways do these two lists facilitate hope?

> What does the image of the New Jerusalem say about the nature of our future relationship with God?

*Note: when reading Revelation it is always good to go for the 'big picture' and ask about the kind of hope/threat in the passage, rather than to worry about details.

Eschatology

The term Christians use to discuss their understanding of the future is 'eschatology', which means, quite literally, 'last things' (from the Greek word for 'the end': *eschaton*). The Christian view of time is linear, not cyclical. History had a beginning with creation (however creation came about), it passes through many millennia, and it will eventually have an end. That end brings not the termination of life, but the consummation of God's purposes in creation.

Biblically, the last things are described using images, symbols and metaphors. The book of Revelation, for example, is a book of symbols. This is one of the reasons why it is difficult to understand, yet it is also one of its fascinations. In the gospels, Jesus refers to this future as the kingdom of God, already present in him, and he describes it using parables.

The church points to the kingdom of God, for it is in the church that God's rule has a foothold on earth. As we discussed in Study 11, God's rule has broken into human existence, but it will not be complete until the old order is completely swept away. This led to our description of the kingdom of God as being 'already and not yet' present. Likewise, the church will not be pure until the end of the age. The Holy Spirit, meanwhile, is given to God's people as a pledge of ultimate salvation and to prepare them for the future with God. This understanding of salvation sees it as 'inaugurated', but not yet fully consummated. It is a view that is therefore called 'inaugurated eschatology': the end is now, even while we wait for its final arrival. This is the sense of the New Testament idea that we live 'in the last days'.

ACTIVITY

Look at the references to the 'last days' in Hebrews 1:2, 1 Peter 1:20, 1 John 2:18. When are they talking about?

The Return of Christ

The full and final arrival of God's kingdom comes with the return of Christ. This event is known as 'the second coming', though the New Testament word for it is *parousia*, which means something more like arrival, appearing or 'presence with', and does not really indicate Jesus 'coming back' to something he left, so much as a new situation: all of creation in the presence of Jesus. This *parousia* of Christ will be a public event in which the world meets the Saviour face to face. When will this occur? Only the Father knows (Mark 13:32–36). Its occurrence will be a surprise. Paul likens it to the coming of a thief in the night (1 Thessalonians 5:2). If someone confidently pronounces the time of the end, you can be certain of one thing: they are wrong.

ACTIVITY

The New Testament often talks about Jesus' coming soon (e.g. the parables about being ready at any time in Matthew 25). How should we interpret this 2000 years later?

The point about Jesus' coming like a thief in the night, or about being ready to meet him when he comes (Matthew 25:6), is not that he was expected to return 2000 years ago and this turned out to be mistaken. Rather, it is a point about how we live in the knowledge that one day we will experience the judgement and grace of God. We live knowing that we could be face-to-face with God at any time. It is about readiness and hope, not timetables.

ACTIVITY

Consider the well-known question: if you were to discover that this was your last day on earth, what would you do differently? Now ask: how does the Christian gospel ask us to imagine using each day for God? In what ways is this similar to or different from imagining what we might do if we knew the world would end tomorrow?

Christ's return brings about the resurrection of the dead and the end of the present world order (and thus also 'the life of the world to come', as the creeds have traditionally put it). It is to our world that Jesus returns to enact judgement, and the purpose of judgement is to set things right in this world. While 2 Peter 3:10–13 describes how the current world order will be destroyed and all of life exposed (or laid bare) before God, this passage also describes the new way in which everything is organized as 'a new heaven and a new earth'. The new order, in other words, is the re-making of heaven and earth, rather than the replacement with some other place (such as a disembodied heaven).

ACTIVITY

Read 2 Peter 3:10–13 and compare it to the Revelation passage at the beginning of this study.

The millennium is the 1000 year period described in Revelation 20:1–6. Its main point, in the book of Revelation, is to indicate that where God's faithful people have suffered and been treated unjustly in the past, they will be vindicated and allowed to 'reign' in the future. It is striking how little is said about the millennium in Revelation, although its main point is important: Christians may hope for evil to be overcome within our creation.

ACTIVITY

Reflecting on your reading of Revelation 20:1–15, how would you answer the question of when the millennium will occur compared to when Christ returns? What might be the significance of this?

Revelation does not answer the question of when it will occur, or when the *parousia* will occur in relation to the millennium. However, this is an important issue for some, so it is worth briefly defining the central views. The view that Christ will return before the millennium is known as 'premillennialism'. Since on this view the period of peace (the 1000 years) does not occur until after Christ's return, such an approach tends to argue that Christians should expect (and in a certain sense welcome) signs of disintegration of our world, since it means the coming of Christ is near.

'Postmillennialism' argues that Christ returns after the millennium: the world will attain a state of peace and then he will come back. This view was more common before the horrors of the twentieth century, world wars and all—it seems harder to maintain now. Since the time of Augustine, it has been common to argue for 'amillennialism'. Confusingly, this is not the view that there is no millennium, but rather that the millennium is symbolic of an undefined period during which Satan is 'bound' and unable to have his full way on earth. On this view the millennium refers to the current age of the church. The age of the church began at Pentecost—which was the view of the early church—and will end with Christ's return. Revelation does not give a clear indication of how to resolve this puzzle.

The Resurrection of the Dead

When Christ returns, the dead will rise to life. As you saw in Study 21, the hope of the resurrection of believers is founded on Jesus' resurrection: just as his physical body died and was raised to new, transformed life, so one day will ours be. The significance of Jesus' resurrection for his first followers was its startling indication that the hoped for resurrection of the faithful (as portrayed, for example, in Ezekiel's image of a valley of dry bones coming to life—Ezekiel 37:1–14), had already begun, and therefore, in some way, the 'end' had already arrived.

The image of the New Jerusalem in Revelation 21 is a way of describing what it will be like to live the resurrected life. It is a joyful and liberated life. In transformed bodies, God's people will be free from the bondage of sin, past guilt and failures. This new existence will be characterized by the life of the Spirit, who even now is preparing us for it.

This idea of the resurrection of the dead often raises a question for people today: what about those who have died already, where are they now? Have they been taken out of time and are already with Jesus? Or are they too waiting? Those who believe that the dead await Christ's return call this period of waiting the 'intermediate state'. This state is temporary, and entails resting with God. While the New Testament does not address this question directly, it does use the terms 'paradise' and 'sleep' in ways that might relate to the idea of an 'intermediate state'.

ACTIVITY

Read Luke 23:43 where Jesus mentions paradise: what could it mean in this context? For examples of 'sleep' in this sense in the New Testament, read Acts 7:60 and 1 Corinthians 15:51. Also look up Luke 20:37–38. What is Jesus saying here about Abraham, Isaac and Jacob, and what does this tell us about the dead?

In Jewish tradition, paradise is a temporary resting place where people are alive with God, awaiting the final resurrection (which was, in the first place, a Jewish idea). The Hebrew term *sheol* offers a related image. In the Old Testament, the dead go to *sheol* after death, where they have a shadow existence. When Saul uses a medium to call Samuel up from the dead, Samuel appears as a spirit and chastizes Saul for disturbing him (1 Samuel 28:11–15).

In Luke 20:38, Jesus seems to be saying that the dead Patriarchs are still alive in God's eyes. While he does not explain in what sense this is true, it makes sense to imagine that they are being described here as awaiting the final resurrection (since the resurrection of believers is the topic of discussion in this passage).

Many church traditions have not focused much on this intermediate state, perhaps as a result of collapsing the New Testament idea of death and resurrection into a single notion of 'going to heaven when you die'. The Roman Catholic idea of 'purgatory', a state where believers go to be purged of any residual sin prior to entering God's presence, is not a New Testament image, but is clearly an attempt to describe one solution to the puzzle about how the dead finally enter the resurrection life.

ACTIVITY

How would you answer the question of where people go to when they die? Are there biblical passages that you can point to which help your understanding? Do you agree with the idea of an intermediate state? Why or why not?

Hell and Heaven

Jesus' return marks the point of 'final judgement'. This has stimulated many graphic images in paintings down through the ages, but it is described quite simply in the New Testament as a separation between those who have chosen God and those who have not. God claims his own, and in the process rejects (and finally destroys) evil.

Traditionally, the concept of 'hell' in Christian thought has been a mixture of ideas of destruction and simply the absence of God. The word 'hell' derives from the Hebrew term *Gehenna*, the name of a ravine near Jerusalem that functioned as a rubbish dump. Fires frequently burnt in this dump, and the bodies of criminals were disposed of there. In the first century, it was the place where the unwanted was destroyed.

Scripture uses a variety of other images to describe this 'hell', including a place of darkness or of 'weeping and gnashing of teeth'. Such images communicate pain, punishment, exclusion and void. Suffering there may be physical, but it is also mental and spiritual. The punishment of hell is directed against wickedness. Hell is the location of godlessness, the place where everything that goes against God's nature is cast. In the end, it too is destroyed (Revelation 21:14).

ACTIVITY

Read some of these images in passages such as Isaiah 66:24, Matthew 8:11–12 and 2 Thessalonians 1:6–9.

The topic of hell raises a lot of uncomfortable questions. For example, how can hell exist if God has defeated evil? Is universalism (the belief that all will be saved, regardless of what they say in this life) a viable Christian position? How long does hell last—is it eternal or is the image of its 'destruction' (Revelation 21:14) meant to suggest that it is not? This is linked to the question of whether human beings are inherently 'immortal', or whether this is a gift given to those who have 'eternal life'. Debates on these questions have been running for centuries, probably because the biblical texts are not entirely clear on these matters.

ACTIVITY

Read some of the passages relevant to these debates. On universalism: how do we hold together 1 Corinthians 15:22, Romans 11:32 and Matthew 24:36–42? On immortality, note 1 Timothy 6:16. On the duration of hell: consider Mark 9:44–48, Matthew 10:28, 1 Corinthians 15:50–54, 2 Peter 3:7 and Jude 7,13. What sorts of conclusions would you feel confident drawing?

In contrast, heaven in the New Testament is simply the place where God is. This is why the newly recreated world can rightly be called 'the new heaven and the new earth': this is one place and not two. There is no longer a distinction between God's dwelling place and humanity's. This separation was marked by the curtain in the temple, which was torn from top to bottom when Jesus died (Matthew 27:51), symbolizing that his death opened the way for God to dwell with humanity.

The holy of holies in the temple was the place where God was understood to be: only the high priest could enter it and only once a year. In 1 Kings 6:20 we read that this space was cubic in shape. Then, when the New Jerusalem is envisaged coming down from the sky in Revelation 21:16, it is also cubic, though in fact huge. This symbolizes that, in one sense, the new creation is now holy in the way that the holy of holies was holy in the temple. Thus, it is the new-heaven-and-new-earth.

Living with Hope

Bible Passage: Psalm 100

STUDY QUESTIONS

What are the characteristics of living for God in this Psalm?

> ➤ What are the reasons given for 'making a joyful noise' to the Lord? (vv.3,5)

> ➤ Different translations give v.2 as 'Worship the Lord' or 'Serve the Lord', because 'worship' and 'serve' come from the same Hebrew word and idea. In what sense can we understand worship and service as two aspects of a single activity? (see also Study 8)

> ➤ Why is thanksgiving linked to entering God's presence? How might this translate to our activities today?

> ➤ Reflect on your own experiences of joy, thanksgiving and praise—when have these been prominent in your life and why?

This final study is different from the others—we will use it as a time to reflect on what you have studied through the book and think about how to put it into practice in the future. You can do this either in a group or on your own, but the key is that it will be your own reflection on how our studies relate to you. This should be a time of encouragement as you consider how your own understanding and vision of God have grown.

Work through the following questions either in discussion or by writing down some personal answers.

- How has your understanding of God the Father changed, and what hopes do you have for the future based on this?

- How has your understanding of God the Son changed, and what hopes do you have for the future based on this?

- How has your understanding of God the Spirit changed, and what hopes do you have for the future based on this?

- How would you describe salvation and what are its implications for your daily life?

- What have you learned about the biblical story and how has this helped you to understand the God who is at work in your life?

- What new insights have you had into how to interpret the Bible? How might you plan to make the most of these in your future Bible study?

- In what ways do you see your own life as part of God's mission to the world around you? Are there practical steps you should take in the near future?

- What does it mean in your own context to live with hope for the future?

- If you had to express in your own words what 'living for God' is all about, how would you now say it?

As with almost all Bible study, theology, and thinking about the Christian life, this book of studies will have raised as many questions as it has answered. It will have suggested things you would like to look into but haven't had time to. At the end of the book you will find a few resources listed that will help you go further.

We are called to live as God's people, playing our part in God's plan as he recreates the universe and brings together all things in Christ. Not all will come to him, and along the way Christian discipleship will be a messy and tiring business, but it is all our response to the great God who has made and remade us. May we, with Paul (in Ephesians 3:14–21), kneel before the Father in heaven and ask to be strengthened with power through his Spirit in our inner being, so that Christ may dwell in our hearts through faith. We conclude with an opportunity to reflect on Paul's prayer in Ephesians.

Bible Passage: Ephesians 3:14–21

STUDY QUESTIONS

What vision of God underlies this prayer?

> ➢ People usually stood to pray in New Testament times. What is the particular significance of kneeling (or 'bowing the knee') here, then?
>
> ➢ How is an understanding of the trinity present in this prayer?
>
> ➢ How does the prayer balance individual and corporate aspects of discipleship?
>
> ➢ What is the significance of what is 'known' in this passage? What about what 'surpasses knowledge'?
>
> ➢ In which two places is God's glory to be seen? (v.21) Reflect on the implications of this in your own situation.
>
> ➢ It is perhaps appropriate to respond to this passage, above all, in prayer and thanksgiving.

Suggestions for Further Reading

For each study unit we recommend one particular book as an ideal place to go for further reflection or discussion of the studies in the unit. If you purchase these books they will form the start of a good Christian library. In each case we also recommend a few other resources, *starting with simple and introductory ones and moving on to more challenging books.* We have tried to keep these suggestions brief and up to date, so that they would be available if you wanted to buy them. There are hundreds of good books on all these topics, and more coming out every year. Two additional notes at the end look at different types of resources available for biblical study, and worthwhile general reference books.

Unit I—Knowing God

MAIN RECOMMENDATION

* Alister McGrath, *Theology: The Basics* (Oxford: Blackwell, 2004)—reviews most of the important issues (wider than just this unit) in a clear and straightforward way

OTHER USEFUL RESOURCES

N.T. Wright, *The Challenge of Jesus* (London: SPCK, 2000)—explores who Jesus is, from a New Testament perspective, with a focus on how it makes a difference today

Richard Bauckham, *God Crucified: Monotheism and Christology in the New Testament* (Carlisle: Paternoster, 1998)—brief but challenging account of how the New Testament portrays Jesus as God

Max Turner, *The Holy Spirit and Spiritual Gifts: Then and Now* (Carlisle: Paternoster, 1996)—thorough study of all the relevant biblical passages

Unit II—The Christian Life

MAIN RECOMMENDATION

- N.T. Wright, *Simply Christian* (London: SPCK, 2005)—a book with a similar goal to our own, to get the basics in view simply but not simplistically

OTHER USEFUL RESOURCES

David Ford, *The Shape of Living* (London: HarperCollins, 1997, with several reprints since)—thoughtful and creative series of reflections on living as a Christian today

Kevin Giles, *What on Earth is the Church?* (London: SPCK, 1995)—a thorough study of the biblical resources for understanding what the church is and does

James Beilby & Paul R. Eddy (eds.), *The Nature of the Atonement: Four Views* (Downers Grove, IL: IVP Academic, 2006)—presents each model in dialogue with the others

Unit III—The Biblical Story

MAIN RECOMMENDATION

- Craig G. Bartholomew & Michael W. Goheen, *The Drama of Scripture: Finding Our Place in the Biblical Story* (Grand Rapids: Baker Academic, 2004; slightly revised edition London: SPCK, 2006)—good overview, focusing on issues of theological importance in the overall story rather than 'what happened when'

OTHER USEFUL RESOURCES

Richard Burridge, *Four Gospels, One Jesus: A Symbolic Reading* (2nd ed, London: SPCK, 2005)—how to read the story of Jesus in four ways but as one story

John Barton & Julia Bowker, *The Original Story* (London: DLT, 2004)—an introduction to the contents of (and the world of) the Old Testament

Ben Witherington III, *New Testament History: A Narrative Account* (Carlisle: Paternoster, 2001)—a straightforward telling of what happened

Unit IV—Interpreting the Bible

MAIN RECOMMENDATION

- Gordon D. Fee & Douglas Stuart, *How to Read the Bible for All Its Worth* (Grand Rapids: Zondervan, 3rd edition, 2003)—goes through all the different kinds of literature you read in the Bible; also contains a guide to good Bible commentaries

OTHER USEFUL RESOURCES

Richard Briggs, *Reading the Bible Wisely* (London: SPCK, 2003)—combines 'how to interpret' material with 'what is Scripture for?' material

N.T. Wright, *Scripture and the Authority of God* (London: SPCK, 2005)—argues that 'the authority of Scripture' is shorthand for 'God's authority —through Scripture'

David Holgate & Rachel Starr, *Biblical Hermeneutics* (SCM Studyguide) (London: SCM, 2006)—a similar 'study guide' format to this book, looking at some issues in how people in different contexts read the Bible differently

Unit V—Mission: Sharing the Good News

MAIN RECOMMENDATION

- J. Andrew Kirk, *What is Mission? Theological Explorations* (London: DLT, 1999)—includes thorough consideration of many different contemporary issues in mission

OTHER USEFUL RESOURCES

Richard Bauckham, *Bible and Mission: Christian Witness in a Postmodern World* (Carlisle: Paternoster, 2003)—suggestive short book on how the biblical 'metanarrative' (overall story) relates to the modern and postmodern world in which we live

David Bosch, *Transforming Mission* (Maryknoll, NY: Orbis Books, 1991)—a classic work, also available in a shortened and simplified form as: Stan Nussbaum, *A Reader's Guide to Transforming Mission* (Maryknoll, NY: Orbis Books, 2005)

Christopher J.H. Wright, *The Mission of God: Unlocking the Bible's Grand Narrative* (Nottingham: IVP, 2006)—major study of how the 'whole of mission' relates to the 'whole of the Bible', not just to a few favourite verses

Unit VI—Christian Hope

MAIN RECOMMENDATION

- Tom Wright, *Surprised by Hope* (London: SPCK, 2007)—a clear analysis of many of the main topics in this unit, concerned to understand the New Testament on its own terms

OTHER USEFUL RESOURCES

Trevor Hart and Richard Bauckham, *Hope Against Hope: Christian Eschatology in Contemporary Context* (London: DLT, 1999)—helpful analysis of the main 'symbols of hope' in Christian thinking and how they can inform our lives today

Christopher Rowland, *Revelation* (Epworth Commentaries; London: Epworth Press, 1993)—one of the best commentaries on Revelation for showing its practical relevance and message of hope for living today

Christopher J.H. Wright, *Old Testament Ethics for the People of God* (Nottingham: IVP, 2006)—a vision for how the Bible drives God's people to live out their faith for the whole of creation; incorporates his two earlier books: *Living as the People of God* (1983) and *Walking in the Ways of the Lord* (1995), the titles of which indicate the overall emphasis

Additional Note 1

RESOURCES FOR STUDYING THE BIBLE

If you are not familiar with the range of materials available for biblical study then it can be a bit puzzling to know what to use. This note is simply to define some useful terms for you.

A **concordance** is a reference work listing major words in the Bible and giving you the verses in which every occurrence of the word can be found. This is very useful for compiling a list of passages to study, and for locating that half-remembered verse about being innocent as doves and wise as serpents. If the concordance is based on a translation, then you may need further help about where the idea or theme that you are studying occurs when it is not translated in the same way.

Some concordances will indicate the link between the word you are studying and the original Hebrew and Greek words it translates. Some go further, and concentrate on the derivations of words, and allow you to look at what the Hebrew and Greek originals meant at different times. These books are sometimes called **lexicons**. You can even get entire theological dictionaries organized by the Hebrew and Greek words, which can give you enormous depth in your understanding of some terms. You do however have to remember the cautions about word studies noted in unit IV.

A **commentary** is a book that takes you through a book of the Bible, commenting on what is being said. There are hundreds of them. A good one should do a variety of things, but most importantly it should answer the question 'What is the text really saying—on its own terms?' It should also provide you with the information you need about the historical background to the book, and things like difficult translation issues that you probably cannot tackle yourself. A one-volume commentary will do all these things a little, but is most useful for providing you with an overall view of the book in question. Use it especially for these overview-type studies. One of the best available is:

- J.D.G. Dunn & John Rogerson (eds.), *Eerdmans Commentary on the Bible* (Grand Rapids: Eerdmans, 2004)

A **Bible dictionary** will give you basic information about a variety of biblical topics, varying over individual books, names of people or places, ancient customs, main theological ideas, archaeological information, issues like chronology or authorship or maybe even ethical issues. This can be an invaluable tool as long as you are prepared to supplement it with your own study.

Another useful practice is to have more than one **Bible translation** available, if possible, which will help you avoid building your interpretations on one particular way of translating a passage. It is good to have one quite literal translation for study purposes, even if you find it easier in general to read a more simply written translation in a modern version of your language.

Many modern **study Bibles** combine quite a lot of these features, and can be very useful for reference, as long as you remember that the notes at the bottom of the page do not carry the same authority as the biblical text!

If you wish to learn **Hebrew and Greek**, there are many good courses available. We recommend the two books by John H. Dobson: *Learn Biblical Hebrew* and *Learn New Testament Greek* (both Carlisle: Piquant, 2005).

The actual texts for reading the Bible in its original languages are the *Biblia Hebraica Stuttgartensia* (eds. K. Elliger & W. Rudolph, Stuttgart: Deutsche Bibelgesellschaft, 5th ed, 1997) known as *BHS*; and *The Greek New Testament, Fourth Revised Edition* (eds. Barbara Aland, et al., Stuttgart: Deutsche Bibelgesellschaft, 2001), known as *UBS⁴*. You can buy Greek and Hebrew Bibles from the Bible Society at www.biblesociety.org.uk

Additional Note 2

USEFUL REFERENCE WORKS AND TEXTBOOKS

Many college and university courses in theology or religious studies make use of textbooks and reference works for the students. Some of these are very useful for looking things up or reading more widely and deeply. The following are all good in their chosen areas. Most of them are very large (and quite expensive), but are reference books to last a long time. They are generally at a more advanced level than the work we have been doing in this book.

TEXTBOOKS

Daniel L. Migliore, *Faith Seeking Understanding: An Introduction to Christian Theology* (2nd ed., Grand Rapids: Eerdmans, 2004)

Alister E. McGrath, *Christian Theology: An Introduction* (4th ed, Oxford: Blackwell, 2006)

Stephen B. Bevans & Roger P. Schroeder, *Constants in Context: A Theology of Mission for Today* (Maryknoll, NY: Orbis Books, 2004)

REFERENCE BOOKS

F.L. Cross & E. A. Livingstone (eds.), *The Oxford Dictionary of the Christian Church* (revised ed., Oxford: OUP, 2005)

John Corrie (ed.), *Dictionary of Mission Theology: Evangelical Foundations* (Nottingham: IVP, 2006)

Sinclair B. Ferguson & David F. Wright (eds.), *New Dictionary of Theology* (Leicester: IVP, 1988)—a revised edition of this is due soon

Adrian Hastings, Alistair Mason & Hugh Pyper (eds.), *The Oxford Companion to Christian Thought* (Oxford: Oxford University Press, 2000)

Kevin J. Vanhoozer et al. (eds.), *Dictionary of Theological Interpretation of the Bible* (Grand Rapids: Baker Academic & London: SPCK, 2005)

Available from Piquant Editions

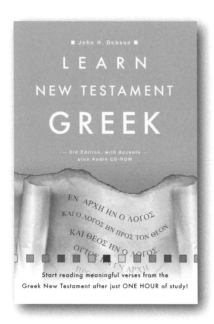

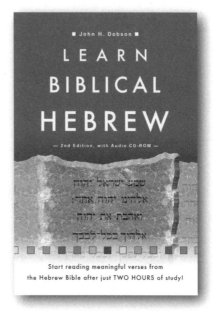

PIQUANT
editions

www.piquanteditions.com